Stanley Nass was educated at Columbia University and the City College of New York. He is on the faculty of the Brooklyn Center of Long Island University, where he teaches in the Department of Guidance and Counseling. Professor Nass is the author of a variety of articles on psychotherapy and the editor of *Approaches to Crisis Intervention*.

Manfred Weidhorn was educated at Columbia University and the University of Wisconsin. He is Professor of English at Yeshiva University in New York City and is the author of three books and of more than two dozen essays in professional journals.

Turn Your Life Around

Self-Knowledge for Self-Improvement

Stanley Nass

Manfred Weidhorn

A SPECTRUM BOOK

Prentice-Hall, Inc., *Englewood Cliffs, N.J. 07632*

Library of Congress Cataloging in Publication Data

NASS, STANLEY.

   Turn your life around.

   (A Spectrum Book)

   Includes index.

     1. Self-actualization (Psychology)   2. Self-
perception. I. Weidhorn, Manfred, (date)
joint author. II. Title.

BF637.S4N37   158'.1   78-15360

ISBN 0-13-933069-0

ISBN 0-13-933051-8 pbk.

The lines from "The Second Coming" from *Collected Poems* by William Butler Yeats are used by kind permission of Macmillan Publishing Co., Inc. and A. P. Watt Ltd.
Copyright 1924 by Macmillan Publishing Co., Inc., renewed 1952 by Bertha Georgie Yeats.

A SPECTRUM BOOK

Printed in the United States of America

10 9 8 7 6 5 4 3 2

PRENTICE-HALL INTERNATIONAL, INC., *London*
PRENTICE-HALL OF AUSTRALIA PTY. LIMITED, *Sydney*
PRENTICE-HALL OF CANADA, LTD., *Toronto*
PRENTICE-HALL OF INDIA PRIVATE LIMITED, *New Delhi*
PRENTICE-HALL OF JAPAN, INC., *Tokyo*
PRENTICE-HALL OF SOUTHEAST ASIA PTE. LTD., *Singapore*
WHITEHALL BOOKS LIMITED, *Wellington, New Zealand*

Contents

v

Contents

Part IV
It's Time to Live 187

Preface

Unhappiness is the lot of man. Psychological research no less than the testimony of literary artists and historical archives seems to render that as near a certainty as any statement can be. Rich or poor, aristocrat or slave, intellectual or illiterate, powerful or exploited, handsome or ugly—no circumstances make, despite the teaching of sages and the preaching of ministers, any dent in that fact of life. No matter how well off one is, the possibility of improvement, the awareness of greener grass elsewhere or tomorrow, spoils one's happiness.

Nor is there any known cure for this peculiar disease. Now, as always, thousands of teachers, mystics, prophets, sages, and gurus preach a single gospel: happiness—how to find it and how to keep it. The difference is the means. Some find it through God, others through art; isolation or teamwork; ritual or social reorganization; prayer or bomb throwing; meditation or activism; abstinence or moderation; psychedelic drugs or macrobiotic food; family life or monasticism; reason or impulse.

Some swear by virtue, but even the virtuous have their

inner storms and stresses and the transience of more hedonistic pleasures such as beauty, sex, food, drink is too well known to require any added comment. Study and wisdom have been celebrated by religious and irreligious thinkers alike as a mainstay, but intellectuals, scientists, artists, philosophers are no more immune to melancholy and madness than anyone else. Most people swear by money, but only because they do not have much of it. Those who do have it know that it can create new problems as fast as it solves old ones.

No, anxiety is part of the human condition. That is why counselors, whether in their ancient role as dream interpreters, theologians, and preachers or in their modern role as psychologists and psychiatrists, have always held a respectable position in society. Part of the folly—and dignity—of humanity is that we accept nothing as final but keep on trying to break out, to transcend ourselves, to find Nirvana.

This book is one such attempt, hardly the first of its kind and hardly the last. The reader will ask: If, as you concede, un-happiness is a fact of life and if we seek a solution that does not exist, why bother reading or writing this book? The answer is that we may have a susceptivity to be dissatisfied, but there are still gradations that make a difference, such as that between con-stant or intolerable and periodic or mild unhappiness. Careful analysis *can* separate insoluble *emotional problems* from easily sol-uble *sloppy thinking*. No book or therapy can free people of the discontent and hurdles of everyday life, but good advice can re-duce unnecessary wretchedness to common, tolerable problems.

With the exception of severely disturbed individuals, who can only be helped by lengthy and expensive professional treat-ment, *most people have small emotional problems and large intellectual confusions*. That is, most people cannot think straight, and their difficulties are caused by *sloppy thinking, not by bizarre feelings and reactions*. Their errant emotions are of the sort that is responsive to reasoning. Their cure can come in a number of forms: therapy; a course in logic; talking to friends; experiencing a great novel, play, or film; or undergoing a startling and therefore enlightening experience. Some of these methods—like therapy—are expensive; others—like reading great books—are a hit-or-miss proposition. You may have to spend hours on many books, certified classics though they be, before you hit on one that has the desired impact on you by dint of touching in some way on your own peculiar problem.

This book is mainly an informal exercise in clear reasoning; it addresses itself to those difficulties most likely to beset the average person. It is more candid than most friends are. Some individuals will, to be sure, still need the prodding that comes from face-to-face talk with others or from communal rivalry in order to change their ways. But those with sufficient will power, motivation, and intelligence to take a trip will find here the one thing they lack—a psychological road map, a psychic itinerary, a compass for the self.

This book is meant to initiate self-examination by providing guidelines, methods of logical analysis, and various suggestions. After reading it, some will find that they still need added, external aid. So be it. Others, though, may conclude that they no longer do. You have to decide in which group you belong.

The average reader's predicament is analogous to an electric machine that is not functioning. The owner opens it, takes it apart, replaces worn-out components—all the time not quite knowing what to look for. Just when the owner is ready to consign it to the repair shop or the garbage pile, someone comes along and points out that the machine is not plugged into an electric outlet. That operation being performed, the machine works as well as always. So it is with everyday affairs. Some people have difficulties that require consultation with specially trained repairmen. The problems faced by most, however, are really matters of simple oversight and poor reasoning, matters that proper suggestions can set right. The absence of even a little insight or piece of advice can make a problem seem large and insoluble.

In offering some rather rudimentary, commonsense observations and remedies, this book performs a function similar to that of the instructions to home appliances. They say that if your appliance does not work, you should, before calling Service, check the following: Is it plugged in? Are all vents and windows unencumbered? Are things like the water faucets properly open and those things that are supposed to be closed, closed? That is all this book purports to perform. But that is a lot.

Many of the counsels in it will come not as news but as reminders. Most people need but to be recalled to what they already learned, need but take more seriously what they know but blithely dismiss. *They will be pleased to learn that the machinery of their daily lives is not broken, but the plug is out, the faucet closed, or the vent covered.* They would be surprised at the extent to which a minor quirk or circumstance throws one off balance—rather as a minor thing like an ingrown toenail or twisted ankle, by forcing one to walk a certain way, can result in pains in knee, hip, and back and can wreak havoc with posture, daily physical training, and mental equilibrium. They would be pleased to see the extent to which some relevant advice, a little consequent adjustment in one's behavior and life-style, will obviate problems that seem large and permanent and will materially improve one's happiness quotient.

Of course, no individual, system of thought, or book should be looked to for the *Definitive Answer*, because none exists that will equally suit the tall and the short, male and female, rich and poor, lustful and ascetic, bookish and athletic, idealistic and cynic, anxious and placid. What we can do is help you ascertain what your goals are and make suggestions that will speed you along. But the basic choices and actions are up to you. Many systems of thought presume to impose universal values on everyone, regardless of differences in temperament and capacity.

Our message is not the preacher's: "Here is the panacea, the magic formula!" but the travel agent's: "You tell me where you want to go, and I'll arrange the mode of transportation, the schedules, and the linkups most appropriate to you." There are a lot of answers—a lot of schedules and itineraries—to be applied with intelligence to varying individuals in varying situations. This book makes no claim to definitiveness. All we can do is provide suggestions, ventilate issues, shed light on old problems, scrutinize answers, offer you a hierarchy of questions and procedures, and leave it to you to apply all that. The very fact that all individuals are unique and can shape their own lives rules out the providing of any simple, universal *Answer*. To give yourself to any ideology is to lose your uniqueness. You must extract from systems of thought what is universally wise or what applies to you specifically.

We present here a simple survey of basic truths, shorn of the philosophical, literary, and psychological associations with which they were first propounded. We present the ideas as they are relevant to current everyday situations, not as they are part of a systematic reading of the universe. Though we seem to grapple with a series of problems, we actually deal with different ways of looking at the same problem—lack of knowledge, of self-knowledge. Turning it as one does a gem in one's fingers, seeing different facets of it, we become more familiar with the problem. You do not know what coffee is, no matter how much you have studied the chemistry, agronomy, and economics of the bean, until you have tasted it. In the same way, merely one version of, one way of looking at, the problem does not give you the sensuous, rich sense of it that you get from a survey of the same problem's manifestations in different forms and contexts.

Trying to be direct, nondogmatic, nontechnical, nondidactic, we do not so much prescribe as describe. We do not so much tell you what to do as explain the options you confront. We do not so much counsel as reveal. We certainly do not claim to have the answers to everything. For one thing, there is grief. The poet Frost said that politics is about grievances, which can be remedied, and poetry is about grief, which cannot be remedied. This applies here; we deal with grievances of the psyche, which can be straightened out, not by legislation, but by reordering of priorities and ways of thinking. But for grief and its causes—illness, death, loss of loved ones, and the like—we can offer no more advice or help than anyone else can. Let time do its work; this too shall pass; look at the larger picture; *che sera, sera*. But such bromides are no shortcut, and your grief must work itself out and run itself down in its own good time.

Although we make no claim to having the last word, we do claim to have rooted our thinking in common sense. We believe in both discipline and pleasure. *Every moral choice is judged by how it helps or hinders you alone.* This book is about and for you, and no one else. We will not tell you to do anything for anyone else. We avoid all talk of duty or responsibility, all "should" and "ought" used with reference to any system or faith.

We begin with the proposition that all people, regardless of religious affiliation or lack of it, idealists no less than realists or cynics, are selfish; that is, oriented toward the self, me first, number one. We accept that as a fact that cannot and should not be changed. *The issue therefore is never between selfishness and altruism but over the results of selfishness—between enlightened, farseeing selfishness and benighted, counterproductive selfishness.* Some forms of selfishness may help others and some may hurt others; but the main question is, Will these forms help or hurt you, me, the person making the decision?

Because hurting someone else often results in pain to oneself in the long run, it is, as a general rule, to be avoided. Steal from someone and you will be caught and jailed. Cheating on an examination may appear harmless to you, but should it lead to your expulsion from college, inability to get references, and vocatìonal ruin, it is to be ruled out as not worth the risk.

Some of our suggestions are therefore going to seem startling, because we express what many people feel but what few ever admit to or express in print. Other instructions, however, will harmonize with the wisdom of the ages. In the latter cases, *we will be suggesting not novel moral choices but novel reasons for making those choices.* Thus the Bible tells you not to kill, lie, and steal because God disapproves. The modern secular moralist tells you not to kill, lie, and steal, because it harms others and injures society. *We* say that you should not kill, lie, or steal, because when you follow through the consequences of your actions, you will eventually find yourself hurt by them. In most cases, the old proverb that "honesty is the best policy" is true, but the equally old proverb that selfishness is evil is false.

A Psychological Self-Examination

Who is Angelic Me?
See Chapter 7.

What is Terminal Habititis?
See Chapter 15.

Are you a Kvetcher?
See Chapter 13.

Should you make lists of Things to Do?
See Chapter 16.

What can be done for Galloping Futuritis?
See Chapter 18.

Can you detect the Child-Person?
See Chapter 5.

Are you governed by an inner Sunset Law?
See Chapter 9.

Where can one obtain Sweet Grapes?
See Chapter 12.

Is Pastitis curable?
See Chapter 19.

Who are the Pregnant People of either sex?
See Chapter 5.

Are there criminal penalties
for the Time Killer?
See Chapter 17.

What is the relevance of
the Principle of King Solomon's Chalk?
See Chapter 14.

How do you cope with the monster Inertia?
See Chapters 2 and 19.

What can looking at things
under the aspect of eternity do for you?
See Chapter 19.

Are you a Conniptor
or do you only dabble in connipting?
See Chapter 10.

Do you walk with psychic crutches?
See Chapter 13.

Should you feel guilty about not
participating in
a sing-along songfest?
See Chapter 7.

Which part of you is like the Thirteen colonies;
which is like a faulty odometer-speedometer?
See Chapter 6.

1

Introduction

Daring to be selfish for a change

For the past few thousand years or so, selfishness has been getting a bad press. Preachers and editorial writers rail against it, politicians campaign against it, people pretend to be free of it. Worst of all, those sufficiently enlightened to be truly selfish are made to feel guilty about it.

To hear most people tell it, hardly any problem in the world cannot be explained away with that cover-all word. Crime in the streets? Dilapidated housing? A useless educational system? The cause is selfish policemen and teachers and politicians and, behind all of these, a selfish electorate. Rising oil prices? Wars? Communist tyrannies and military dictatorships? The problem is selfish Arab sheiks and world leaders. Difficulty in getting admitted into graduate and professional schools? If only selfish admission committees would stop restricting entry into the

1

professions. If only the selfish Blacks would stop trying to get everything out of the liberals and politicians. If only the selfish arms manufacturers would stop milking the Pentagon and Congress. If only farmers stopped hiking their prices and big oil corporations stopped gouging the average worker.

It's always the other guy who is selfish, of course; not me. I'm just doing what's right by me and mine. Sometimes I may do something just to please me, not the teacher, the parents, the boss, the wife, the kids, the pals. After all, I have a little coming to me, too, once in a while, don't I? But most of the time I do what's right, and if all those other guys out there acted like me instead of being so selfish, the world would be a better place in which to live.

That is the general view of things, and, as is often the case, the general view is wrong. The truth of the matter is that the root of most evils is not selfishness but ignorance. Most of us are too unaware of ourselves to be selfish. We try to look after "Number One," but we don't acknowledge to ourselves what it is that we are up to, and that is the first sign of unawareness. We do not know how to go about being selfish, and that is the second sign. We think ourselves wicked for even wanting to be selfish, and that is the third kind of unawareness.

Saving others while saving yourself

To begin with, we should clear our minds of misconceptions. Attacking selfishness is to imply that there is such a thing as *non*selfishness. Yet anyone who takes the trouble to consider even briefly the ways of the world will quickly realize that *all* acts are basically selfish.

"All?"

Yes; every last one, no matter how altruistic it might seem.

"Show me."

Fair enough. See that young man campaigning for a clean environment? He spends all his free time attending meetings, writing letters, speaking in front of community groups, and picketing factories that contribute to pollution. He is so busy arousing the public to the dangers of pollution that he is neglecting his school work, has stopped going to the movies, and is losing weight as a result of his rushed schedule. Is he selfish?

Yes. That young man has decided what is the most important activity for him. Clean air is of vital concern to him. A clean environment will allay his fears about the possibility of falling victim some day to respiratory ailments and cancer. The reduction of pollutants in the air means that he can take better care of himself without the fear that his own health is beyond his control.

In addition to the health benefits, his activities provide him with social rewards. The attendance at meetings, the organizing, and the picketing throw him into contact with like-minded individuals. It is a chance for him to make new friends and exchange ideas.

All right, you say, that young man may have ulterior motives. How about people who risk their lives for others? This fellow over here, the one with the civilian police citation for organizing neighborhood safety patrols: His citation mentions how he saved three old ladies from muggers at the risk of his own life. Isn't calling such a decent, patriotic hero "selfish" carrying cynicism too far?

No, we don't have to call him selfish. Better than putting labels on him, we should examine his actions. Of course, he wasn't selfish in the sense that when trouble started, he ran for cover like everyone else. But selfishness is like ice cream; one person prefers chocolate above all else, another vanilla, and yet another—there's one in every crowd—pistachio marshmallow. In selfishness, as in ice cream or in sex, there is no accounting for taste.

Some people are selfish during danger in that they think only of saving their skins. Others are selfish in that they seek out danger for fear of being considered, or having to consider themselves, cowardly. They have a strong need to be self-sacrificing, proud, and heroic. Perhaps they had stern parents who made such demands of them and turned them out that way. For them to run for cover would not be selfish, but self-lacerating, psychologically suicidal. They would never again be able to face anyone else or even themselves. So doing the dangerous and heroic thing is for them the easy way out, the selfish thing.

"All right, forget about the hero as well as the environmentalist. But what about that college student who spends her evenings and weekends going into slums and tutoring deprived children? Renouncing social activities appropriate for a young woman her age and money, she has devoted herself to hours of devotion to children. Surely she's not to be called selfish as well?"

Why not? In the same way as the others. The helping of underprivileged and neglected children, like protecting others, is the one activity that excites some people, even as playing baseball, tinkering with sports cars, or winning elections excites others. Each activity, fulfilling some inner psychological or physical need, makes one feel good and is therefore selfish.

As for the hard work and the long hours—difficult they may be, but not for that reason unselfish. All athletes put their bodies through intense punishment but enjoy deeply what they do, or at least the end results of their regimens.

As for that woman's devotion to children, who knows where unselfish behavior ends and unconscious attraction begins? By turning herself into an individual trying to help small children acquire the skills for a useful life, that young lady has made herself needed by many. For her to spend instead most of her free time socializing or at some commonplace job would be torture and unselfishness. She finds serenity as the one indispensable person in the lives of many. She is the one who will help these kids turn out well. She can thereby have her cake and eat it too.

So it is also with the other alleged altruists—the reformers and revolutionaries, the teachers and doctors, the public servants. All are doing what comes naturally. Either they like doing what they do, or they like the fringe benefits of the job—ordering people around, making important decisions, having people grow silent and stiff when they enter the room. Or they do what they do because they somehow got trapped into doing it and now have no way out. "Altruism?" "Selfishness?" That's more than we know.

Relax: Others are as selfish as you

What, then, is the point of this rummaging through people's motives? How does it apply to you? Very simply. You cannot solve your problem until you analyze and define it. The problem is not what you thought it was, and the result can be summed up in one word: Relax.

Don't worry about "selfishness." Don't let them— whoever "they" may be—make you feel inferior in the name of "selfishness." Don't let ignorant or hypocritical parents, teachers, clergymen, editorialists—all these holier-than-thou types and spiritual con artists—make you feel as though you are a rotten stinker who in a world of noble souls stands out by caring only for yourself.

If anything is clear from even an elementary analysis of the world around us, it is that we're all in the same boat. The big secret is that few know this fact either about themselves or others. Or they disguise that fact nicely. *Or one person's selfishness is not particularly appealing to another and therefore does not look like selfishness at all.* But selfishness is the name of the game and the only game in town. It's the one common denominator uniting all people. It is, like money, in itself neither good nor bad. It is too general and abstract to be attacked. It is a natural reflex action. To call someone selfish makes as much sense as accusing that individual of breathing.

If everyone partakes of something, no one person can be guilty of it. If the thing is as natural as sneezing or walking, it's not a problem. Of course, sneezing in another's face or walking away with stolen property *is* a problem. But that's not sneezing or walking; that's rudeness or theft.

So it is with selfishness. Certain kinds of it are distinctly reprehensible—either in themselves, or for what they do to others, or, above all else, for the discomfort they cause you. That kind we'll have to discuss. But instead of calling them "selfishness," we'll call them by whatever name is more appropriate.

So stop beating your breast, and give your overworked conscience a badly needed and well-deserved period of rest and recuperation. You may be doing a lot of things wrong, and we're going to try to get at some of them in this book, but selfishness is definitely not one of them.

As a matter of fact, in order to make sense of your life, you must learn to be as selfish as you can. You must learn to lead your own life and stop following others. Feeling guilty about selfishness is silly when not being selfish is simply conforming to others.

The one thing you can ever become an expert on is you. On a lot of other things, you may think or pretend you are an expert. But only on yourself can you ever have real expertise. To do so, you must turn selfish, think of everything with reference to you first, become a student and a professor of yourself, as only you can be. No one else, as a folk song has it, can do it for you. So dare to be selfish—and to enjoy it.

Just Who
Do You Think
You Are?

Some turn to a self-help book because they are having trouble coping. "Trouble coping" can mean anything from being unable to step on cracks in the sidewalk to being unable to ask a member of the opposite sex out for a date. In fact, anything that comes easy to one person may be troublesome to another.

The person so afflicted asks of book or therapist, "Cure me of my psychological ailment." Philosophers say that meaningful answers are elusive, because the questions they respond to are usually unclear. As with computers, you get out what you put in; an answer is only as clear as the question has been.

The same applies to the request, "Cure me of my ailment," which actually harbors two questions: "What's wrong with me, and how can I change that?" What makes both explicit request and implicit question difficult to handle is that there is no single cause; what ails someone is a symptom, a part of something bigger. For the basic problem is not this disability or that hang-up, but self-ignorance.

Who am I?

This statement will surprise most people. "What? Me not know myself? You're crazy! You *may not know yourself, but if there's one thing* I'm *sure about, it's* me. *I know what I like in food and athletes; I know when I like to go to sleep and what sort of movies, politicians, and TV stars I like. Nobody, not even my spouse, knows as well my views on Nixon and Reggie Jackson and Johnny Carson. If I don't know myself, who does? Is there a parent, friend, teacher, or psychologist who spends as much time with me as I myself do? Me not know myself?"*

Not so at all. As with many things, the obvious is not true. People forget that self-knowledge does not consist of thousands of facts stored away in the mind. It consists rather of such nebulous things as one's feelings, wishes, dreams. Besides, the closer we are to something, the less clearly and objectively do we see it, and this applies to nothing so much as to one's self.

"Who am I?" is therefore a question far more difficult to answer than you suspect. "John Smith" tells us nothing; the name is a mere label. Looking in the mirror reveals only the mutable, physical facade to be found at any given time. You see there, in any case, only what you want to see; people in front of mirrors and cameras are notorious for improving themselves, removing their eyeglasses, turning their best sides to the light. What they see in the mirror and photo cannot possibly be what others see every day.

Ask others who you are? People will see only the parts of you that they like or hate. You will get different descriptions from different people. You may be putting on a show for them without your realizing it; so their testimony is untrustworthy, without their realizing it. Or they may be trying to curry your favor or to needle you. Besides, psychologists have shown that people note and remember only those portions of their descriptions that flatter or irritate them.

Look inside yourself? You will find a great, ever-changing river of emotions, impulses, unfinished thoughts. Sometimes you think yourself good, sometimes bad; sometimes heroic, sometimes cowardly. Which are you essentially? Look at old letters and diaries, and you find discarded selves like the skins of snakes— selves you hardly recognize or have anything in common with. You might as well plumb the ocean, count the stars, or collect last year's snows as find out "Who am I?"

The basic problem that people suffer from is lack of self-understanding, and from that ignorance come all other forms of ignorance, such as not understanding others. Often it is easier to cure the symptom than the cause, to understand others than to understand oneself.

The first section of this book delineates four kinds of false assumptions people make about themselves: the illusion of inferiority, the illusion of superiority, the feeling of isolation, and the feeling of belonging.

Just about all of us—except possibly the Napoleons of the world at one extreme and Bowery derelicts at the other—think ourselves fundamentally inferior to most people around us and, concurrently if inconsistently, just as fundamentally superior to them. Everyone likewise feels painfully isolated and different from all others in some crucial and invisible way and, in other moods, feels joyfully a part of a club, clan, party, group, nation, religion, or some other entity and therefore not at all alone.

The very fact that the same individual can entertain such contradictory ideas is the best evidence, if any is needed, that people do not know themselves.

2

You Are Better Than You Think

The Illusion of Inferiority

POOR ME

Everyone feels inadequate at some time, and many people feel that way a good part of the time. The apparent evidence is all around them. This man is president, that one is a rock superstar with a following of groupies. Here's some skinny little kid no one would play with in my high school, and now he's the best lawyer on the East Coast; there's a woman classmate from college who's just won the Engineer of the Year award. Here is your next-door neighbor who won a scholarship to an Ivy League college.

On the other hand, there's poor old you, barely having accomplished anything. It's always the other guy at parties who comes up with witty remarks that set the guests laughing uproariously and who gathers the other guests around himself, while you sit there conscious of your isolation and unable to enjoy yourself. It's always the other guy who—when a fire breaks out or a mugging takes place—

comes to the rescue, calls the police, and throws the malefactor a half nelson, while poor old you just stand there, scared stiff. It's always the other guy at group discussions, class, or meetings who makes a spellbinding speech laced with references to Schopenhauer, Mark Twain, St. Francis, and Marshall McLuhan, while you are awed, jealous, and self-hating. When it's your turn to say something, you begin with a lot of "er. . . er" and then come up with some platitudes that you hate even as you hear yourself pronounce them.

ONLY A FEW CAN STAND OUT

But did you consider that in any group, by the laws of nature and of averages, only a few can stand out? Even those who stand out cannot do so in every field. The witty one is probably a duffer on the ball field; the articulate one is not a very good thinker. So even they know feelings of inadequacy. Only the very few excel in most things, and at the same time there are also others who are less well off than you. At least you did get invited to the party, did get to make a speech.

Odds are that you do not consider this. By observing other people's successes, you believe more deeply than before that you are an inferior, inadequate individual who never realized the great promise with which you started out.

Inadequacy in thought

COMPARING OTHERS' ACHIEVEMENTS WITH YOUR THOUGHTS

That is inadequacy gauged by achievement, by externals, by measurement with competitors. But failures of that kind are in a chicken–and–egg relationship with inner, psychic failures. Without realizing it, you make the case against yourself worse by comparing others' *actions and achievements* with your *thoughts*.

Disreputable thoughts?

Your inner life consists not only of reveries of wished-for, superlative feats but also of disreputable thoughts, thoughts that you barely admit to yourself of harboring: thoughts of jealousy, sex, revenge, self-pity.

You are jealous of others who have made it in one way or another. You would rather say, "Sure, he's great, but he cheated," or "He's not so great. I don't know what you see in him." You will say anything, in short, except what you really think, which is, "He's great, and I'm jealous it's him rather than me." Your mind is filled with this resentment, pettiness, and ungracious acceptance of loss and defeat.

Then there is sex. Most people spend many hours thinking about it. You may mentally undress attractive members of the opposite sex you meet during the course of each day's business, see down the street, or watch in a movie. You imagine how sex with that person would create an unequaled orgasm. If you are in love, you think often of the beloved in sexual situations. If not in love, you indulge in pipe dreams of what that shadowy beloved would be like in bed.

If such thoughts might be considered degrading, others are considered forbidden. You think of getting revenge, physically and psychically, on your enemies. Since such behavior is out of place in a modern, rational civilization, you never acknowledge to anyone the existence of these thoughts; but your mind, never fully modernized, still rampages with the lusts and frailties of the caveman.

Or, when things go particularly badly, you think of suicide, indulge in self-pity, and dare the world to get on without you. Asking people to take no notice of you, you thereby try to extract the maximum possible attention.

Stop! It's not as bad as all that

K NOW YOUR COMPETITOR

The truth is that those feelings of inadequacy are untrustworthy. People do not know themselves. They have weak and strong points and rarely know one or the other. The first thing to realize is that you never see yourself objectively but always under the pall of some mood or other. The other person, moreover, may not be as great as you think. Many put on a display that is better than what the packaging covers.

Some are helped along by the way people choose to think and talk about them, a current that has a great impact on the way you regard them. The flow of beautiful women through that man's front door causes people to think of him as a Don Juan, and what they think rubs off on you. Yet few know that the women initially flock to him because he spends a lot of money on them but do not stay with him because he has an obnoxious personality. This young woman with a fine singing voice—who realizes that once she stops singing and begins to talk, most people find her dull and boring? Here is a doctor with a sparkling office manner, handsome face, large clientele, and good reputation because of his handling of wealthy people and occasional successes in difficult cases. Less well known, however, is that in many run-of-the-mill cases, his attention wanders and his cure rate is low.

So the first lesson is that many people are not as great as everyone thinks they are; nor as great as they themselves think they are, because they are also subject to the rule that no one knows himself. *The corollary is that you are not as bad as you think you are, for you have been comparing yourself with a shadow.*

Are you your own shadow?

But you should set aside not only thoughts of other people and their real or alleged achievements but also the unrealistic ambitions you had or have of being the world's greatest. *Only when you have put unrealistic, impossible demands out of your system, can you begin to work on the possible.*

Using all your resources

"Work with what? What's left?"

Much. Psychologists tell us that most people barely use five percent of their resources in the course of their lives. Entire regions of the mind remain barren, uncultivated. For all we know, there may be dozens of Shakespeares, Martin Luther Kings, Reggie Jacksons, Abe Lincolns who never gave themselves a chance. If you feel inadequate, it may well be because you, *as presently constituted,* are in fact inadequate in some areas. What is important, though, is that *you are not forever so constituted; you are not inferior in essence.* You've merely chosen to let yourself go personally or intellectually the way other people let themselves go in the waistline.

One way out of the trap of feeling inadequate is to start explorations. Not in the South Pole, the Amazon valley, or Siberia, but in a region more remote and unknown than these—the world of your own untapped resources.

Try painting. Try developing your own photographs. Have you ever thought of learning to play a guitar or recorder? It's easy, you know. Work a little more on your handball or tennis instead of giving it up too quickly. How about reading a book? It doesn't have to be something you have associated ever since grade school with work, dullness, torture. It can be on anything that takes your fancy. If you are still in school, how about exploring new fields during the summer and holidays?

Remember that you're not taking a course now. You are a free person, free to follow any subject that interests you. Remember how you felt, as a small kid, that dull and oppressive school work interfered with your life, even interfered with, as a college wisecrack has it, your education? Well, what have you been doing with your freedom? Get up and use your time to pursue your languishing curiosity and interests.

One little step

How is reading a book on, say, the Founding Fathers going to relieve feelings of inadequacy?

By itself, not much. But it is not "by itself." It is part of something, the start of something. When you were a kid in school, you covered a lot of subjects, most of which interested you only minimally. Some, like the Founding Fathers, did so more than the rest. Busy socializing, however, busy with homework and extramural athletics, you had no time to do anything about that interest. You told yourself that when you could find the time, you would read up on the Founding Fathers. Came summer, and there were other summer routines.

The interest is still dormant within you. Turn to it now and see what happens. You may read a book on a subject and find that that about exhausts all you want to learn about the matter. Chances are, however, that it may lead you to another book on the subject or on a related subject, which will lead you to another book, to a trip to a museum, to more books. Before you know it, the mere act of reading a half-dozen or dozen books has started making you an expert on a subject. Suddenly you know more about the Founding Fathers or, as a result of slightly changing interest or emphasis, about the American Revolution than most people.

You have, in short, found an area of excellence. *In at least one thing, you are no longer inadequate.* And yet all you did was to follow up finally a curiosity you had. Without your looking for it or realizing it, moreover, you had a good time in the process.

You say you don't like to read books? There is no reason in the world why you must read them. Try something else. How about photography? Let us say that you have always had a hankering to develop your own pictures but never got around to it. Try it now. Read up on it, or take an evening course in your community school. Before you know it, you will have an expertise, a field in which you excel your friends and neighbors—even while putting together a fine collection of photographs and slides and, not least, enjoying yourself.

There are thousands of such potential interests waiting for you to exploit them. The trouble is that you may have never given yourself a chance, never found out what you are capable of and how flexible life can be. If you are not used to self-scrutiny, try such visual aids as diaries or letters you wrote, autobiographical essays in your English courses, high school and college yearbooks, photographs, tape recordings. Or try conversing with old chums, parents, kin. Try anything that may help you remember interests that are now buried inside yourself.

Though you may think that all options are closed, the world is actually wide open to you. Look at the problems facing someone behind bars—and look at the long list of people who have found themselves under those distressing circumstances, who have become writers, lawyers, revolutionary leaders. *If they could cope in jail, surely you can do at least as well in the comforts of your home.*

GOING DEEP OR WIDE

Once you have subjected yourself to self-scrutiny, you may find that the problem is not that you are specializing or, conversely, spreading yourself thin but that whatever you are doing is not working for you now. The remedy must fit the problem.

The specialist

Let us look at some cases that may apply to you. You may be an accountant or an engineering student, and numbers are all you know. You are a success at your job and studies, but a flop socially. At parties you clam up, because you don't know a thing about current art, American foreign policy, the Italian cinema, punk rock, Latin American life-styles. You are not much of a dancer.

What you need to do is stop reading numbers day and night and cultivate new interests and tastes. Turn from technical books, and begin reading books and magazines devoted to entertainment, sports, arts, and leisure.

The Renaissance man

Or your problem may be that you are interested in everything—that is, in too much. So when it comes to reading, you dutifully read many magazines and books and newspapers, section by section, page by page.

A consequence of this may be that you grow discontented with yourself and feel inferior because of spreading yourself too thin. You know a little about everything and nothing much about anything. Maybe you should cut down on your reading in the *Arts* and *Travel* sections and concentrate more on the *Sports* and *Business* sections if that is your thing—or the other way around. Maybe you should make the reading you do more interesting by accompanying it with readings in books, visits to museums or athletic contests, conversations with like-minded people. If your main interests is sports, forget about the *Real Estate* and *News of the Week* sections. *Stop trying to become a Renaissance man;* few have the capacities for that. *Become rather yourself!*

OVERCOMING THE MONSTER INERTIA

The obstacle to change is that great monster, *Inertia*. This is the grand enemy of all self-improvers. Laziness, fear of the unknown, reluctance to experiment, entrapment by habit—these are the causes of inertia. Grab all these causes by the throat and choke them. Scrutinizing yourself, probing your resources, doing something about your weaknesses and inadequacies—that is initially hard and painful work. Doing nothing, however, will prove to be more disconcerting. And once habits are dislocated, however painfully, the options open up, and the process of liberation becomes easier.

Take the plunge

Keep in mind that nothing in this world is perfect. You may never come to know yourself through and through. You may have difficulty finding precisely "your own thing." You may well be distracted by limitations of time and family responsibility. But one thing is clear: If you keep it up, however imperfectly, you will be a changing person, which is no common thing. It will happen sooner than you realize. Just take the plunge. You have nothing to lose. If the water is too icy, you can always resume watching your favorite TV shows. Don't worry about them. They will always be there; you can rely on that. Rather, *worry about yourself. Where will you be?* Can you rely on that? *Where do you want to be? What are you prepared to do about it?*

Now you know

The nature of the cure depends, then, on your ailment. The steps are simple enough:

1. You are unhappy because
    a. you feel inferior and inadequate and
    b. you do not know where you are going, and you do not like it when you do know.
2. You have first to realize that your priorities and habits are confused, because
    a. you don't know yourself and your strengths and
    b. you don't know others and their weaknesses.
3. You have then to realize that you live in a world of numerous possibilities, both outside yourself and especially inside you, and that you are flexible.
4. To do something about that, you have to
    a. stop worrying about others,
    b. get to know yourself better, and
    c. rediscover your interests.
5. Then you have to do something about these dis-

coveries, by devoting time and energy to your newly found interests and, above all, by breaking your unproductive habits.

3

You Are
Worse Than You
Think

The
Illusion of
Superiority

How special I am!

Feeling inadequate and inferior is some people's problem
or everyone's problem some of the time. At other times,
people think that they are better in every way than others.
Insofar as this perception matches the reality, that person
leads a relatively contented life. But many who think the
same way are clearly not better. They are likely to have
problems, or to create them.

Even today, after all the strides in civil rights and the
general thrust in America toward the expansion of legitimate rights, many white male or female Americans, looking at the illiteracy and crime rates in the ghettos and indifferent to the social causes of such symptoms, believe
that black people are inferior. Many males, black or white,
believe that women are, notwithstanding evidence to the
contrary, inferior physically and intellectually. Many West-

erners of either race or sex believe that the people of the non-Western world, being technologically backward, are in some basic way inferior.

People think this way, not only about groups other than their own, but also about individuals from their own group. Always aware of the deficiencies of others, they ignore or cannot face their own weaknesses and faults.

THE FEELING OF SUPERIORITY

But how can we claim that most people have feelings of inferiority and feelings of superiority at the same time? The answer is that there is a logical and psychological connection between them. People who feel inferior cannot live with those feelings all the time. They therefore take refuge by coming to see themselves superior in other ways. The alleged inferiority even turns out to be a disguised superiority: "What do you mean, I don't know anything about subject X? Subject X is garbage, and the less I know about it, the better off I am!" The reasoning behind it is that if you fail in one way, at least you succeed in another way. And what you succeed in matters more than what you fail in, so you are not bad off, after all. The failures actually aid the fantasy of being superior. Hiding your inferior side, you try to impress yourself on others as superior, and then you come to believe your own propaganda.

Compensation

What starts out as deception turns into self-deception; what began as a "line" for "them" becomes a belief for you. This procedure, known as "compensation" in psychology, may make you able to live with yourself. But it also makes you intolerable to everyone else.

In itself, the procedure may even be a healthy response. If you're weak at football and good at baseball, you stop playing football and work at baseball, where you may truly excel. But when the sense of inferiority is based on lack of self-awareness and the sense of superiority is based on serious self-deceptions, watch out! Trouble is inevitable.

Thus it was that many people in Germany had that curious mixture of inferiority and superiority. Especially after World War I and its attendant disorders and sufferings, many Germans felt like the accursed race of Europe, the most downtrodden, exploited, and victimized. Soon enough, they started believing all sorts of lies about their own racial superiority to this or that group.

The indisputable evidence

Here are some ways that you convince yourself of your superiority. You stress the following traits: common sense, sense of humor, sense of decency, sense of immortality. You also convince yourself of your superiority by believing that you are really better than the way you appear right now.

COMMON SENSE

Who of us do not pride ourselves on being abundantly endowed with it? Who does not say to himself, "Sure, I'm no deep thinker or specialist. I don't have a lot of books read or degrees earned. No elected official comes and asks me what I think about this or that policy. But there's one thing that I can say for myself and that others have to grant me: I've got common sense. I may not know much about foreign policy or economics or books, but I sure can tell a pig in a poke. I know what's important and what isn't."

Since common sense is an uncommon thing, taking pride in it is to set oneself apart as superior. It is at the same time a put-down of all those other people who, not seeing things the way you do, obviously lack common sense. Being the only one able to pinpoint the simple, obvious things in life, the basic moral and spiritual necessities, the practical way of getting through each day, is something many pride themselves on.

SENSE OF HUMOR

Another common source of pride is a sense of humor. Practically no one thinks of himself as humorless. Most people are prepared to admit that they cannot tell a joke without spoiling it—their timing is atrocious, their memory imperfect—but if there is one thing they have, it is a funny bone. They can laugh at funny things, appreciate jokes and witticisms, look out for comic relief, enjoy the incongruous perspective on things. It is no good pointing out that many people are rather humorless and, lacking a sense of irony, often take umbrage at jokes, teasing, half-meant remarks, and the like. People simply think that that rule applies to others and not to themselves.

DECENCY

A third trait that most people pride themselves on is decency. They will admit that they may be abusive to their spouse, parents, brothers, and sisters; that they get angry with teachers who give them low grades and policemen who give parking tickets too quickly; that they are intolerant of criminals; but they are sure that they themselves are decent. If they take a hard line with their parents or spouse, it is because they feel for them and are doing it for their own good. Deep down, they have a very decent attitude toward people, and it is only the few rotten apples among humanity that they are fed up with. Sure, you may go through red lights late at night, cheat on exams, and try to duck traffic summonses; but on the basics, you are a decent person, one of the few in this corrupt world.

The immortality trip

Another kind of superiority everyone has is a sense of immortality. No one acts as though death were an important fact in the future. Many people are, to be sure, haunted by hypochondria and fear of death. This state of mind, caused perhaps by some traumatic experience in childhood, is helped along no little by the bombardment of advertisements. We are to watch out for the danger signs of, and support the mobilization against, cancer, diabetes, tuberculosis, syphilis, muscular dystrophy, heart disease. . . . Such campaigns, however well intended and necessary, cannot but instill immoderate anxieties in people.

Still, anxious though you may be of disease and death, another part of your mind proceeds as though no such anxieties exist. You make your long-range plans, build your expectations, visualize yourself living into old age. Though you know that you will die and even fear death unreasonably, you act as though deep down you feel differently. Death remains an abstraction, a concept, something remote from the flesh-and-blood events from which mathematicians compile averages. You know the chances of being felled by heart disease, cancer, auto accident, or crime; but until it happens, you are in the lottery of life. You say, I have plenty of time in which to relate to my friends, parents, brothers.

This illusion comes from an inability to face reality. Some secret wish becomes the father of the thought that you are immortal. It is helped along by the complacency caused by near misses. You notice this friend or relative coming down with kidney disease, that one involved in a car accident, here somebody battered in a mugging, there somebody in a plane crash or house fire. These are people in your own circle of acquaintances, not celebrities in faraway Hollywood or Paris written up in newspapers. And you even see yourself having a close escape of one kind or another. But as long as you survive and these acquaintances do not, you think you see an emerging pattern whose message is, "You are immune and lead a charmed life. It is no accident that your closest friend got it and you did not. That's because you're charmed to live to a ripe old age while your friend is not."

Of course, if that pattern breaks down and the next close call gets you, there is no problem, because you will not be around to tell yourself that you made a mistake and are mortal after all. If it does *not* get you—and even serious illness and accidents do not count if you survive to laugh them off—you feel justified in making that inference; and the longer you live, the more near misses you have, the more of your friends and relatives die, the more charmed you think you are. Simply living on is like a self-fulfilling prophecy, a self-generating illusion. You shrug your shoulders and decide that such tragedies are for

other people; as long as you are alive, they always happen
to others and not to you. There is a mysterious sense in
you that you have a better destiny than others, are immune
to mortality, *are superior to others in the one thing that
counts—life*. You ignore the likelihood that many of those
friends and relatives who died prematurely also harbored
such illusions, until mortality happened to them.

BEING SUPERIOR TO YOUR JOB AND COLLEAGUES

People think of themselves as special not only in the
biological sense of being destined to live forever or at least
to a ripe old age but also in a vocational, psychological
sense. You may believe that the job you hold now is not an
impressive one, or that the school you are attending is even
less impressive, and that viewed against the background of
your childhood expectations and dreams, it is the least impressive. Many do not set out expecting to attend a technical school or junior college or to be an accountant, a clerk
in the traffic office, a cab driver, a worker on an assembly
line, or a receptionist. Yet cab drivers and assembly line
workers are needed by society to do the necessary jobs.
The type of training that you want and need to advance
yourself may only be found in a technical school or a
junior college. Society has very few openings for opera
stars or major league players, and the size of the freshman
class at Harvard is limited.

Your present situation may be exacerbated if you
haunt yourself with thoughts of your imaginary expectations. So how do you come to terms with your dissatisfaction? *With feelings of superiority*. You tell yourself that you
are far greater than your title and position suggest or the
school you attend. You are a diamond in the rough, a

genius who has yet to be discovered. Naturally, that illusion becomes harder to hold onto as you get older. But illusions are tenacious, and people die still harboring them.

I am better than I seem

To convince ourselves that we are really superior to the way we presently appear, we fabricate illusions about ourselves. The illusion that we possess undiscovered genius; the illusion that we could always do better if we only tried; the illusion that what is happening now is only temporary; and the illusion that next time will be the moment of greatness.

THE UNDISCOVERED GENIUS

One of the four major forms of the illusion is to believe that you are an undiscovered genius, merely awaiting the day when a talent scout will bring you to achievement and recognition. You have in you the Great American Novel, the ability of a home run champion or a Nobel Prize winner. The exact nature of your great talent may still be vague, and the manner in which it will come to fruition and then to public notice is even more vague; but something is clearly there.

IF I ONLY TRIED

A second form of the illusion is to believe that you can do everything much better *if only you tried*. The trouble is that your boss, teacher, colleagues, pay, working conditions are not of the sort to encourage you to do your best.

You feel that you are surrounded by mediocrity and mediocre expectations, and doing one's best would not be recognized. So why even try? You lie down on the job, do just enough to get by, and allow your true potential to go to sleep. If you only tried, you could easily change all that; but there is no incentive for trying.

I AM ONLY DOING THIS FOR THE TIME BEING

This in turn brings in the third form of the illusion, namely of holding a lousy job only "for the time being." Of course, your work is degrading, but as soon as you get the chance or as soon as you have saved up enough money, you are splitting. Then you will do your own thing, write the Great American Novel, or perform some other feat of pure genius. Your present job may seem to the outsider to be a dead end and you—insofar as you are stuck here for years—a born loser; but that is not the case. You have definite plans to alter careers; you cannot give a specific date yet, but you soon will. Many a life has gone down the drain, many a defeat has been accommodated to, in the name of "for the time being."

I WILL HIT THAT HOME RUN YET

Then there are the subsidiary pipe dreams, such as that you have the potential to hit a home run with the bases loaded and make a spectacular, game-winning catch. Even if in reality you strike out, the fantasy merely reasserts itself. "I was rusty today. Next time, you watch me belt it out of the field." No number of actual strikeouts can destroy the fantasy of the sensational home run. No number of times in which you peter out with a lame stammer can snuff out the fantasy of telling off the boss and walking out on the job with shoulders ten feet high. Because whatever you would *like* to have, you tell yourself you *potentially* have. You confuse the wish with the fact, the potential with the actual, the *would be* with the *is*.

Face yourself

The point of all this is this: *Just as in order to make sense of your life, you had to discard the many illusions of inferiority and inadequacy, so must you concurrently discard the parallel and coexisting illusions of superiority.* To go on living with and fostering these illusions is to set yourself up for a catastrophe when they come to clash with the facts.

You are good, but not *that* good. You are decent, up to a point, but so are many people; you, like they, are likely to have your limits.

As for the common sense you pride yourself on, remember that it is not all that common and that it is relative in any case. One person's common sense is another's lunacy, and what you take to be good thinking on your part may well be to others merely thinking along accepted, tiresome, or rash, irresponsible lines.

If you want, in short, to cope and flourish, it may be helpful to see yourself as you are, with only as much decency, common sense, and humor as the next man or woman; to see yourself in fact as *being* the next man or woman, the typical, average person. And the world is run by the average person. Look around you; if everyone believed that he was better than the next person, nothing would ever get done.

The irony is that having once confronted your self

and admitted your kinship with others, you may begin to improve or prosper or, at the very least, to live. Shedding the illusion and pipe dreams is getting a monkey off your back. The *prospect* of facing the facts about oneself is far worse than the actual *process* of doing so. You cannot, in any case, mend until you see yourself as you are—not so special but in need of improvement, active, present, self-improvement.

It may well be that you will leave the unsatisfying job for wider horizons only when you stop telling yourself it will happen and begin telling yourself it won't *happen and start therefore doing something about it.* God, as they say, helps those who help themselves. And they help themselves best who see themselves as imperfect creatures, not as superior, and who accept themselves as they are, neither the lowest nor the greatest.

4

You Are and Are Not Alone
You Are like Everyone Else

The illusion of being alone

One of the things that make individuals unhappy is the thought that they are just that, individuals. Feeling alone, you believe that you have problems unlike those facing anybody else, and "nobody knows the troubles I've got."

It is pretty clear that life is unfair and that some people get a pretty bad shake and some get a pretty good one. Common sense no less than observation suggests, however, that most people are in neither extreme category. They get good breaks and bad breaks, and the two tend to balance out. The thought that bedevils so many people—"I'm different!"—turns out, by the very fact of its ubiquity, to be wrong. *Everybody is different, every person an exception*—and therefore no one is.

Under scrutiny, even the particular differences may turn out to be a common plight. One person is different because he or she has difficulty relating to the opposite sex—so do thousands, perhaps even millions of people. Another has difficulty breaking loose from parents—so do millions of others. One person has problems because of never being able to hold onto money; easy come, easy go. So do many others. Another is shackled to a compulsive saving that prevents him or her from enjoying life. So are others.

The importance of this realization is that your case is not hopeless. Because you think yourself suffering all alone from a rare psychological affliction, you fear that there is no known cure, no interest in your case, nothing to be done. To know, by contrast, that your problem is shared by numerous others is to realize, first of all, that you are human and within the range of normality. You in fact share your plight with a group of people with whom, were you to meet them, you could exchange much familiar information and tips on coping. That is reassuring news.

So relax. You share your particular problem, however difficult it may seem, with others; and in having a problem, you are like everyone. Shocking and even a little disillusioning as it may sound, you are not so special after all!

The illusion of not being alone

The reminder that you are not alone must, however, be coupled with the one that you *are* alone. A contradiction? Of course, and not the first one you have encountered in life. But it only seems to be a contradiction. The point is that you are alone in some ways and not alone in others.

Deep down, humanity is aware of, and dreads, its isolation. We are—each one of us—separate particles, and our ultimate experiences—birth and death—are journeys we must take alone. You try to hide that fact from yourself in many ways. You join political parties, patriotic groups, religious sects, social clubs, in order to make yourself belong to larger entities. Belonging to a group gives you a sense of being not just an individual but part of an intricate web. Having families of your own who depend on you to earn a living and run the house is not enough. You feel the need to increase the web of connections, the range of your associations. So you join other forms of extended or substitute families, like a church ("all men are brothers") or a fraternal organization (*frater*=brother). Membership in each group reassures you as to your identity, your belonging to something, your playing an important role in the life of others. It enables you to say, "Sure I know who I am—I'm John Smith, and if that name is too common, I'm an Episcopalian, Republican, Rotarian, Little Leaguer—or a Catholic, Democrat, Italian–American, Knight of Columbus."

Most people dread those rare moments when they are not relating to anyone else. Those are just the moments when one might become aware of one's ultimate solitude. So you try as far as possible to lead a life of never being alone—school or work, then off to meetings of the various organizations you belong to, then socializing or family life. That is why people have difficulty coping with increasing leisure time and retirement. "Not having anything to do" is simply another way of talking about being thrown back on one's own resources, confronting the fact of ultimate individual loneliness.

Fortunately—or unfortunately—modern technology has made it possible for people to live their whole lives without ever facing themselves or the facts about themselves. For now, when those relatively rare moments of not being with others come along, you are saved from yourself by the distractions of mechanical companionship— provided by records, radio, and television. Now you need never be alone. Through technology, we are all now one happy family—or so it seems—and you can take refuge in the illusion of not being alone. ˒

Conformity

A more important kind of sociability is moral rather than physical. It involves not so much *being with* people as *acting like* them. That is "conformity": doing things as others do them; following the lead of others; keeping up with the Joneses. People are conformists in good part because they are rendered anxious by their loneliness. They cannot bear to think that they stand out in any way, even in exercising intelligent choices as an individual. That is why many people prefer to vote and think like their relatives, friends, and colleagues. There is comfort in knowing that you are part of a large group, preferably the largest.

Some forms of conformity are good and important. By conforming, we learn our three Rs in school. By conforming, we make life easy for ourselves and others. Manners and etiquette, for instance, involve conformity to a set of rules that are sometimes arbitrary and meaningless but that grease the machinery of everyday life and make it possible to get through the day with a minimum of stress.

Conformity allows the game—whether of baseball or of life—to be played with a minimum of fuss. So, if you are getting into trouble because you make a fetish of individualism, you are making a mistake. The following are examples of misguided individualism.

Reinventing the wheel

A misguided individualist exists in every crowd. He is the fellow who has to run around with hair uncombed, beard unshaven or untrimmed, baggy old clothes. He refuses to do something not because it is wrong or harmful but because it is expected of him and everyone else does it. He will not abide by grammar and spelling in his writing; he will not go through such formalities as standing up for the national anthem or saluting the flag. He will not remove his hat, pay his respects, or make polite inquiries and perfunctory compliments. "I'm different, original, unique, sincere, authentic!" he insists.

What is wrong with him is not the idea he espouses but his misapplication of it. To be unique is laudable; to be so in trivial matters is trivial, foolish, and sad. It is a distraction from the important individualism. The person who makes a big deal out of not observing the rules of spelling and grammar is so busy reinventing the wheel that he has no time or energy left for modernizing the automobile or inventing a superior mode of transportation; no time left for composing sentences that are forceful, pithy, and memorable.

Philosophizing

The person who asks why three strikes constitute a strikeout in baseball may be raising an important philosophical question. He may even turn out, with the passage time, to be a prophet or reformer, the sort of man who examines assumptions everyone else accepts unthinkingly and who thereby leads to a revolution in thinking. Or, as is much more often the case, he may turn out to be an eccentric who is ignored by his acquaintances and bypassed by history.

The point is that asking why three strikes is a strikeout is perfectly relevant in a graduate school seminar on the meaning of athletic competition and perfectly irrelevant at a sandlot where a bunch of your friends just want to pass the afternoon with a relaxing game. You may think you are a genius, but your friends will think you are a crank and, rather than let you spoil their day, will play without you. So what did your nonconformity accomplish? It did not lead to an overhaul of baseball. It did lead to your missing out on a nice, friendly game.

Discarding convention

So it is with conventions about neckties. If you insist on discarding a silly convention, fine. But if you do it in the middle of a funeral or wedding, you are showing terrible taste in turning attention from the bereaved or the delighted to you, who are merely a guest; or if you are the groom, from the celebration of the occasion to an irrelevant issue. If you do it on an interview for a job, you may be striking a great blow for liberation from the tyranny of neckties, but a blow that will have no consequences other than your not getting the job. You are calling attention to your eccentricity and making sure that your *best* talents will *not* be paid any attention.

You must learn not to make an issue of things like

spelling, or how many strikes make a strikeout, or wearing neckties. You must learn to subordinate these matters—which have been settled long ago—to important things like writing a powerful story or essay, hitting a bunch of home runs, and achieving greatness in your chosen field. Some of the most revolutionary, individualistic people have been outwardly conformist, shy, and deferential but in their methods of thinking or their modes of action, as subversive as anyone could be. On the other hand, many a nonconformist in spelling or dress has led a vacuous, uncreative intellectual life and gone to the grave unknown.

One can go further and maintain that you *cannot* even *not* conform, no matter how hard you try. Even if one revolts, one conforms. The question is not, as it is often mistakenly put, to conform or not to conform. It is rather what to conform to—to society or to some sub- or counterculture. But conform you must. People who dress sloppily, as rebels long have done, are certainly not conforming to the fashions of polite society but are conforming to the fashions of some other society—of bohemians, Beatniks, Hippies. *They may say that the latter sort of conformity is superior to the former kind; they may not say that they are free of conformity.*

Anyone who observes the mores of the dropouts quickly notices how conformist they are, not only in dress but in eating habits, morality, politics, religious cults, and the rest. Indeed some critics even remarked that the counterculture was merely a mirror image of the society it was rebelling against: By making a fetish of how one dressed and what one ate, by judging people on whether they drove a large new Cadillac or a battered old Volkswagen, it aped—if in reverse fashion—a society hungup on fashion in dress, food, and automobiles.

Complete nonconformity is, strictly speaking, an illusion and therefore no goal at all. Relative, modified, or sensible nonconformity is legitimate but should be separated from the empty-headed, time-wasting kind that makes the most noise and busies itself over means, trifles, and technicalities.

Nonconformity

If those whose compulsion to not conform—a compulsion that gets them into trouble rather than dignifies their lives with creativity and achievement—have to be told to cool it and pipe down, other people need prodding in the other direction. They need to be made to see the virtue, and sometimes the necessity, of nonconformity. If in small things conformity is a blessing, in big things nonconformity is a good all too lacking. *Many people do not have to be told to conform; they have rather to be told not to conform so much.* In their anxiety over loneliness, over standing out, over being different, they eagerly join this cult or cling to that faction and lose all individuality. They vote and think like the people they associate with. They think that they are acting out of their own convictions, which supposedly rest on a solid and tested foundation of fact. They are merely acting out of the group's convictions, however, and have had their minds made up for them by the preconceptions and prejudices of the group.

RUNNING WITH THE PACK

Some people become enslaved to "them"—whoever "they" are—by making a fetish out of dressing fashionably in order, as they mistakenly think, to get things from others. A few small minds may be impressed by such antics, but most people will be either indifferent, see through it, or, most commonly, judge the individual upon his or her ability and effort on the job, not on social conforming. To dress slovenly may cause your talents to be lost sight of amid the outrage and ostracism, but to go out of your way to dress expensively and fashionably will not necessarily get you far, either. To try to make superficial things like clothes do what substantive things like talent and intelligence cannot is doomed to failure. It may even boomerang, for you will be seen for a phony.

An example of conformity among "chic" people is the obsession with the first-run movie. A new film comes out, and—as a result of good reviews, word of mouth, a big publicity campaign, or any combination of these— suddenly everybody flocks to it at once. It is common to see these people, on a blustery, bitterly cold winter night, for as much as an hour in a line that runs around three blocks.

If they but had a little patience, they could see the film a month or two later for half the price and a year or two later free on television. The movie may, in any case, often turn out to have been overrated by critic, grapevine, or publicity puffery. Yet next time around, those lines will be right back there. This is conformity with a vengeance: to undergo all this merely to be able to say to one's crowd, "I saw it. I liked it, did you?" and to be spared the humiliation of saying, "No, I haven't seen it yet," or even, "No, I haven't seen it." To refrain from seeing it would be to stand out of the crowd, and no one wants to do that. The crowd will protect itself and its conformity by labeling you *not* as individualist but as a loser, someone who gets the word late and is just not "with it"—or as a snob.

Some people may brainwash themselves with such put-downs of you in order to reassure themselves of their supposed superiority. It would be silly and self-destructive of you, however, to adopt such put-downs, to see yourself in such a negative light. Let them do their nonsense, but you know better. Let them spend their lives being puppets pulled about by the strings of conformity and racing from one nonevent to the next, pretending all the while that they are having a good time.

Hence, if an important first step in the recognition, diagnosis, and treatment of a particular hang-up of yours is for you to see that you are far from being the only one suffering from it, an important second step is for you to be reminded that you are, after all, a mature individual with your own life to lead, your own problems to solve, your own values to apply. Similar though you may be to many others in your group or clan, you are—in accordance with the Western religious and the secular American democratic traditions—unique.

Establishing your uniqueness

You cannot begin to make your way out of your predicament until you see that as an individual occupying a particular time and place, you are like no one else. Hence no one else's values and prescriptions can apply to you completely. It's all right to listen to the advice freely given you by parents, clergymen, friends, teachers, psychologists. It is all right to *listen*. But you must ask yourself if it applies to you.

All advice givers are blissfully unaware of varying circumstances. Take just one relatively unimportant-seeming item, the birth sequence. One does not have to be much of a seer, beyond being an attentive parent or sensitive child, to note that the world looks quite different to the first-born child, especially son, than to the second or youngest born. The children are treated differently; their characters and perceptions are shaped differently.

First-born children are used to being the apple of their parents' eye, to carrying responsibility, and to being looked up to by the siblings. The only child is used to solitude, to doing things alone, to seeking friends outside the home earlier and more intensively. The second child, from the time of birth, shares attention with another child. Throughout childhood, he or she has a pacemaker; there is always a child ahead, and he or she is stimulated to catch up. Thus the second child learns to behave as though in a race. The last born is used to being spoiled, condescended to, victimized, and deferential.

These are important albeit invisible and overlooked factors in the shaping of the personality. They are also good reasons why one should not conform blindly to others' ways of doing things. *Parents may be the third or youngest born, addressing themselves—without full comprehension—to problems peculiar to the eldest born or to their only child.*

Not only one's place in the pecking order matters, but the time span as well. Not only being younger matters, but how much younger. And that in turn changes with varying periods of life. Thus a sibling who is only one and a half years younger may at a certain stage have a harder time of it than if he had been three years younger. When the older one is five, the younger one—at three and a half—may not have matured sufficiently to have developed a clique of friends his own age and may be tagging along with his older brother and *his* friends, among whom he will become the football, whipping boy, and all-around victim. Had he been three years younger, he would not have been let out of the house on his own and so would have been spared such humiliations. At other ages, notably in earlier childhood and in adulthood, the differential between being one and a half years younger or three disappears. To say therefore that one's character is shaped by whether one is the oldest, youngest, or in-between child does not cover the problem enough. How much younger and what sort of stages did one go through in one's relations with siblings?

Yet in assessing others, though people are immediately conscious of the other person's ethnic background, religion, social class, and economic bracket, they rarely include birth sequence as a category. "Don't listen to him, he's a Pole/Italian/Catholic/Jew/rich lawyer/WASP snob." It could well be, however, that all first-born sons have more in common than do all Irish Catholics, that you may have more in common with a fellow first-born son of a Jewish family than with the fourth child of an Irish Catholic family like your own.

OUT OF STEP—THE CONSEQUENCES

Birth sequence is merely one of many invisible groupings and categories. There are also circumstances like being left-handed; being bookish in an athletic household or, conversely, athletic in a bookish environment; being melancholy or extroverted; being homosexual or asexual.

In all cases, the individual out of step will be under tremendous pressure to conform. The advice proffered by people will be plentiful, the tolerance they will show will be limited, and their unwillingness to sympathize and learn will be only too obvious. The individual may be consequently headed for neurosis and dislocation.

If she yields to the pressures and conforms, she will be acting according to guidelines that are irrelevant to her. She will be a hypocrite, an outsider, a cynic; a devious, secretive, unhappy person. She may therefore turn out to be a great inventor, artist, writer, adventurer, politician, revolutionary; or she may grow up to be a malcontent, never quite fitting into any environment, either of job, family, or community.

If, on the other hand, she is strong-willed and combative, she will fight her family and community on each issue, insisting on her right to be herself. Whether she succeeds or finally knuckles under, she will have an abrasive, iconoclastic personality, a tendency to view life as a battlefield. She too may grow to be a creative person, but she too is more likely to end up a sorehead, the village atheist or radical.

Advice

You must assess the advice given. One person's counsel often conflicts with another's, and what are you to do then? Is the advisor dispassionate or possessed of an ulterior motive?

PARENTS

Take your parents. They love you very much, and *they may believe they best express their love by making you resemble themselves in every way possible.* With the best of intentions, therefore, they sometimes screw you up. This is a problem to watch out for. "Honor your father and mother," says our culture, and we all feel indebted to our parents for begetting and raising us. They made us what we are—even though we may not be entirely satisfied with the end product. And such reverence is no doubt proper, up to a point; respect is due.

Evaluating the advice

In receiving advice from them, however, you must ask yourself if what they think is good for you is in fact so. You are not—need you be reminded?—they; and they are not you. They may be your flesh and blood, but their experiences differ greatly from yours. The generation gap yawns wide. What, for instance, do grandparents or parents coming of age in the Great Depression or the Cold War have to teach their children coming of age in the affluence of the 1950s and 1960s or the détente of the 1970s? Much of what they say can be a helpful reminder of the other side of the coin, and equally much will be archaic and irrelevant. *They are alive in the later decades as much as you are, but they only know what it means to be young in the earlier period.* A respect for money and savings is a value worthy of being passed on, but not in the same form it took for those growing up in the Great Depression or World War II. For the child growing up in a society of relative prosperity, credit cards, and chronic inflation, it makes more sense to buy things than to let the money dissolve in a savings account. Listen to their advice carefully, therefore, but keep your distance, reserve your judgment, make up your own mind.

To your parents you are always a child

When they try to impose their values—religious, political, or moral—on you in your adulthood, it is time for you to remember that you are no longer a child but an adult. *The period in which they "know better" is, for better or worse, over.* You have your own life to live. Don't let them make you feel guilt-ridden about your insistence on independence. You have, in most cases, little to feel guilty about. Sure, they worked hard and sacrificed, but they knew what they were getting into, and they liked having kids. They derived pleasure from raising you. You were not—though they sometimes speak that way—a burden to them who owes them everything now.

GOING YOUR OWN WAY

You are grown up and have the same rights that they have to a life of your own and as they had *when they grew up and moved away from their parents.* The option you face is of having it out with them or going along with their demands. An unpleasant choice. Still, you are an adult and you have to have it out. You must stake out your position. You should not fear them as if you were still a child.

Parents who attempt to force a son or daughter to follow in their vocational footsteps, against a child's expressed desires, may think that a little bit of advice and pressure will change their child's mind. But you know you must go your own way. You have to keep reminding yourself *not to feel guilty over going your own way.* No one need conform to the wishes of parents on matters about which they are wrong.

CLERGYMEN

Clergymen have made a great commitment of energy and emotion to a particular value system; and in some religions they have also committed—that is, foregone—their sexual lives. Their advice is therefore likely to be shaped by that powerful commitment, *that constant need for reassurance that their self-discipline was not in vain.* If that is your need as well, if you are ready to make a like commitment, well and good; listen to them. But if you are not exactly where they are, be careful of what they say. It simply may not apply to you. Don't expect them to see that it does not. That is for you to discover. *You alone are responsible for your own life.*

TEACHERS, FRIENDS, AND PROFESSIONAL COUNSELORS

Your teachers, friends, and professionals are likely to be less pushy about these matters than your parents and clergymen—which means that for some people, *they are the more dangerous.* Since the parents and clergymen may come on too dogmatically and demandingly, there is no danger that you—with your individuality and even a streak of perverseness—will blindly follow their advice. Friends, teachers, and professional counselors, on the other hand, are more objective-sounding and considerate. This difference in tone can easily mislead you into thinking that there is a difference in the worth of the advice being offered.

Be careful of the manner in which the advice is given. The truth—or at least good advice—can be offered in an objectionable way by obnoxious characters, and bad advice can be offered in exemplary fashion by charming and gracious people. Just because acquaintances offer help in a nice way is no reason for you to suspend your skepticism and adopt their values. Their lives may be beautiful and gracious but remain *their* lives, not yours. You must see for yourself where they are and where you are. Then think and act accordingly. No one can do it for you.

Individualism and freedom

Now that you know that you are neither alone nor that you can avoid being alone, that conformity is both a necessary civilizer and a shackle on individuality, that you should go along with the crowd yet be scrupulously dissenting, you can see that the proper response is most nearly akin to a juggling act. By traversing a narrow path between the sense of inferiority and the sense of superiority, between conforming and not conforming, you will somehow capture those rare birds, *Individualism* and *Freedom*. You may fail, but the prize is worth the risk.

WHAT TO DO WHEN TRAPPED

1. Take stock of yourself, and decide whether you have the will, the mettle, the endurance to fight it out or whether you would flourish better by yielding on externals and being an inner exile.

2. Having made that decision on the basis of your own strengths and weaknesses and not on the basis of what others want from you, stick to it. Don't give up, don't look back, don't compromise.

3. There is no need to perpetuate either deviousness or combativeness. Set your goal on achieving independence as soon as possible. If your parents or colleagues do not like that, you have to make them see that they

created an impossible situation for you. The sooner you get out of that unhealthy tension—unhealthy not because it is tension but because it results in continuous deviousness or struggle beyond the point of diminishing returns—the sooner you get into an environment where you can be yourself and act free; and the sooner, the better.

4. Don't feel in the least guilty about doing that. All children must, if they are to mature, break away from their parents (as well as teachers and childhood colleagues) sooner or later. Those with an uncongenial, hostile environment must do so sooner.

5

The Child Is Father of the Man

Justified feelings of inadequacy

About some feelings of inadequacy, little can be done; an unattractive, insensitive, inept, and impoverished person is in for a difficult time, no matter how many religious cults and self-help therapies that individual turns to. Anxiety—another common term for feelings of inadequacy—is, as theologians and psychologists remind us, built into human nature and ineradicable.

Human beings must simply get used to the fact that whether they win the lottery, achieve a mystic experience, marry the most beautiful/handsome girl/guy on the block, or get elected unanimously President of the Universe, they will have periods of melancholy, find woolens itchy, be annoyed by boring people, become sleepy at the wrong time, and worry about trivia for worrying's sake. The human mind will remain divided, with opposing voices in it. Sleep will be disturbed. Human worry over what the next day will bring remains the only constant in our mutable existance.

Pregnant people

Besides these permanent feelings of inadequacy, however, exists a series of others that—transitory, baseless, foolish—are perhaps amenable to treatment. *They are caused by your having no clear identity of your own*, by being consequently not selfish enough, or not selfish wisely enough.

In your daily routines, you take on various identities and roles. Many are not of your own making. *They are the burden that the past places on you.* "The child is father of the man," said the poet. Since children are impressionable creatures, much that happens to us when young stays with us as adults. This includes archaic and obsolete ways of confronting life that were deliberately inculcated in us, no less than much that happened to us then by accident. It means that some bad habits of our elders have been instilled in us and that certain phases that children go through have remained with us because of circumstances that did not allow us to grow out of them.

CHILD–PERSON

The adult who readily gives way to temper tantrums and hysteria over trivial points: Look carefully at him or her, and you see a child in an adult body. When that individual was a child, temper tantrums would immediately yield up parents and thus satisfy this individual's need for attention. Or take the indecisive person. Parents told us what to do when we were young. So did teachers and camp counselors and older kids. Some people remain arrested in that phase and are unable to act without being told what to do. Those who are alert can easily see in many other ways the child lurking in an ostensible adult, the child–person.

LIVING WITH PAST GLORIES

The person who as a child was obese and never did learn how to dance, as did all his or her classmates, still feels self-conscious on the ballroom floor, long after the obesity has been shed. Conversely, those persons who were charismatic as children by dint of athletic prowess often go through life with a sense of something seriously wrong, because life does not turn out to be a football or basketball match with clear-cut rules and simple virtues. They cannot accustom themselves to ordinary lives. They still feel as though they were football stars, fading back for a pass. Whatever happened to the team spirit, the cheering crowds, the adulation of the fans, and the Homecoming Balls?

IMPRESSING OTHERS

Then there are the people who are what sociologists call "other-directed"—anxious over the image they project. One reason they try so hard to impress others is that that is how they were brought up. Parents urge on children the importance of *appearance*, of combing hair, keeping clean and neat, worrying what the neighbors will say, making others love or fear us. As people were taught in childhood, so do they believe and live in adulthood—neurotic, fear-ridden.

DEPENDENT ADULT

Or there is the woman who lived in heavy dependence on her father, perhaps as the first born and best loved or as the only child. Her dependence carries over into adulthood. She marries a man who will shield her from many of life's realities as her father did. She expects things of him that other women would not expect from their husbands. She cannot see that, though her husband may bear some resemblance to her father, he is ultimately a different person and that their marital tensions spring from her inability to acknowledge any difference. Thus it is that the outlook and actions of the mature person are a petrified version of the child. *Many people of both sexes are permanently pregnant people, carrying within them the children they once were.* For some, that is a very heavy burden.

INEPT ADULT

The person who grew up in a home where manual dexterity was not at a premium and who never saw his father repairing anything is likely to be equally inept. He is used to running to a mechanic for any little problem. This will keep his hands clean but may cost him hundreds of dollars annually in avoidable repair fees. Instead of telling himself, as he always does, that he simply was not born with mechanical aptitude, he must come to see that the allegedly innate ineptitude merely grew out of his environment and upbringing and can be changed. He should devote his energies to changing that. He can have the satisfaction of doing his own repairs in addition to saving considerable sums of money. (Some repairs will, of course, have to be left to professionals, but many tasks will not.) Much that we ascribe to nature and genes is really a matter of conditioning; much that we ascribe to fate is really a matter of choice *or lapsed choice*. We simply do not give ourselves a chance, because we let the past dominate us. *We are ruled,* said an Italian seer, *by the dead.*

The long dead hand of the past

Here are further examples of how the past has shaped our present. Remember those feelings of inferiority discussed in Chapter 2? The psychological roots of this curious put-down of yourself are not difficult to understand. People are not born inferior. They are made so. And it took a lot of time and effort by those around you a long time ago to do such a good job on you. Through the magic of self-fulfilling prophecies and vicious circles, it became easy.

OVERBEARING PARENTS

It might have begun with your parents being too overbearing, insensitive, demanding. They may have been successes and been unable to suffer fools, unable to tolerate failure, especially in their own home. Or they may themselves have been failures, resentful of that, and intent that no child of theirs would repeat that miserable record. The result was the same inability to put up with failure.

Whatever the reason, when as a child you made an error, dropped something, or were slow to learn, they made you aware of your inadequacy and made you feel incompetent. Such rebukes scar a child's soul—so much so that when you went out to play with the kids down the block or to study in school, you dragged that psychic abuse after you the way a kite drags its tail. The other kids—children never being much known for sensitivity or tact—sniffed weakness the way a shark smells blood in water. They went after you. Having made a mistake or two, having had that mistake blown out of proportion by your demanding parents, you were on the way to becoming the local sad sack. There is nothing some kids like to do better than to tie tin cans on the tail of a cat or of a sad sack. So the torrent of abuse, contempt, and derision poured on you from friends and classmates.

Teachers

Teachers are supposed to be more understanding and supportive of underdogs, and many are. Others, being human and with their own childish streaks, have their attitudes shaped by the way the children comport themselves, the way the others take to them, and the way the children's parents do or do not support them. So some teachers take the easy way out by perceiving you the way your parents, classmates, and now even you yourself see you. Result: more failure, abuse, guilt. Low marks in school.

Labels

"Stop being so clumsy, you oaf!" bellow parent and teacher. Clumsy? You spilled some Coke once or twice. An insensitive parent or uncaring teacher manages to turn that into a national tragedy. Or, "You did it again! What's wrong with you?" "Wrong?" you say to yourself; something *must* be wrong with me, because they say that time and again only to me. Or, "When will you ever learn and grow up?" When, indeed?

Once you are labeled as "clumsy" or a "nebbish," you are done for. *People will see you that way even when you show no trace of it. But you will show traces of it, partly because we tend to live up to expectations and to the labels placed on us and partly out of a masochistic desire to curry favor with those rejecting us by being just what they expect and want us to be.*

Finding the self

So here you are in adulthood, feeling inferior, left out, a loser, unable to cope. And you wonder why! You simply forgot your past; you blocked your painful childhood out of your memory. Once you revive and review it, the miracle is not that you are browbeaten and feeling inferior but that you survived at all.

In order to live well now, therefore, you must find the true self, the real you. You must psychically, give birth. You must dispose of the past by seeing that you frequently act on roles shaped for you by your childhood fears and by the adults who then dominated you. This involves rummaging through the baggage of memories, tracing actions and values to their roots in the early years, and coming to see those roots as childhood experiences whose relevance has passed, childhood responses that can now safely be let go. You must shed the world of the fantasies and dreams of other people imposed on you in childhood and further distorted by the fantasies of your peers and Hollywood. You live in the present by seeing the roots of your behavior in the past and disposing of that past as best you can, rather than letting it hover over you. Only by making your behavior as independent of the past as you can will you be living in and for the present.

You are in fact pregnant with twins—with the child that you were and with the mature, developed adult you have the potential of becoming. As you go through your everyday life, these twins fight for mastery. As long as you wallow in inaccurate assessments of yourself and indulge in sloppy, incoherent thinking, the child-that-you-were holds sway over you and in effect has come to birth. But once you see yourself properly, straighten out your thought processes, and take charge of your life, the adult-you-could-be takes over from the child-you-were. It comes to birth by becoming the real you. You must, in short, separate the childish you from the adult you by nurturing the latter and letting go of the former.

You have to change others' attitudes toward you

The remedy is not easy. Simply finding out how you got here will not do the trick. You are going to have to undo the decades of brainwashing, bad habits, and bad publicity you have had. Even if through some wonder drug you changed yourself overnight, it might still take months or years for the word to get to your acquaintances. Were they *not* to see you acting in your natural inferior manner, they would merely assume that you were undergoing a brief interlude. *And as long as you have not changed their attitude to you, you have not or cannot change your own self-perception.* So you face quite a task. But you cannot even begin to undertake it until you realize your true position and how you got here. That is the beginning of wisdom. So go ahead; start looking at your own past by way of finding your true self in the present. Is it any wonder if that face in the mirror has been saying to you so far, "Just who do you think you are?"

II

If You Only Knew!

Placing yourself on the psychological map—finding yourself among the mountains of superiority feelings, the valleys of inferiority feelings, the swamps of feeling unlike everyone else, the forests of trying to act like everyone else, and the quicksand sucking the mature-you back into the child-you-were—is only one problem. The solution of that problem is rendered difficult by an even bigger obstacle: humanity's basic and continual unwillingness to confront the truth.

The idea that the truth will makes us free is perhaps too optimistic, but the truth at least helps us see where we are at. That may be precisely why many people prefer to evade it. They suspect where they are at, and they mistakenly think that if they close their eyes, the world will not see them or find them out. For a while that dodge may work, but eventually one is engulfed and defeated by the march of events.

There is no limit to the ingenuity people bring to the act of keeping the truth away from themselves. The reason seems to be

61

*that the mind is not yet, at the present stage of human develop-
ment, a unity. It is rather like the Thirteen Colonies right after the
Revolution: They had enough in common to break away from Eng-
land but not yet enough to come together into a confederation;
each state at first went its own way. Thus can one dodge the truth
because the memory tends to go its own way and to offer pictures at
variance with what originally went through the senses.*

*Another effective barrier to comprehension is the human
habit of punishing the transmitter of the truth as though the
transmitter were the cause or ally of it. No less frequent—and
harmful—is making everyone adhere to a set party line as to reality and penalizing those who refuse to do so. A most important dis-
torter of the truth is one's line of work or dwelling place, for what
you see depends on your vantage point and the angle from which
you see it. Also problematic in ascertaining the truth is the nature
of the assumptions you start out with. How much do they stand on
facts and proof and how much on that great impersonator of facts,*
habit?

*Put all these things together, and you have a prescription for
potential disaster. People are putting these things blithely together
every day of their lives. No wonder they have difficulty coping.
Smith, for instance, has a lump in his hand and goes to one doctor,
who says, it is cancer; remove the hand. Smith obtains a second
professional opinion, which is that it is just a benign tumor; no
need to do anything about it. An intelligent person would get a
third and possibly even a fourth professional opinion; but some
people—who knows how large a minority or majority—have had
the terrors thrown into them by the first diagnosis and therefore
adhere to the second with irrational elation and blindness. The
second opinion removes the death sentence, soothes their vanity as
to personal immortality, and, above all, spares the immediate hor-
rible prospect of having the body hacked. But sometimes, alas, the
more bloody solution may be the right one; sometimes a part of the
body must be sacrificed that the rest may live.*

In the short run, the truth may indeed hurt, but that initial pain at least prevents catastrophe later on. Avoiding the slight pain of the truth now merely lets one in for disaster later. No human being can or should be brought to live with the truth in every way, but periodic injections of it can help one straighten out.

6

Let's Face It
—You Won't

The
Elusive Truth

Wishes as reality

An assumption most people make is that whatever is in one's mind at any moment is the truth—that is, a reflection of reality, of the way things are. That is the biggest illusion of all, one that encompasses many little illusions. *For what is in one's mind is not a carbon copy of reality but a shopping list of one's wishes.* Most people believe not what is *out there* but what is *in here*, those desires packed away in orderly fashion like sardines.

EXPERIENCE AS REINFORCER OF ILLUSIONS

But don't experiences, events, facts make a difference?

Not really. *Experience does not knock down the illusions you harbor so much as reinforce them.* You are selective in your exposure; you screen out all experiences and data that would cause disruption; and if they get through anyway, you interpret them in such a way as to fit in with what you believe. It is nearly impossible to dislodge an illusion. They have a way of perpetuating themselves, and you cooperate in their insidious survival. You hug them to your bosom.

MEMORY PROBLEMS

What helps the process of evading the truth is that the memory is an unreliable instrument. Imagine driving a car with a faulty speedometer and odometer. When you are in a residential area, you cannot tell whether you are exceeding the maximum speed of 25 miles per hour; when you are on a superhighway, you cannot tell whether you are going at least the minimum permissible speed. With an erratic odometer, you cannot tell much about the car's past: Does the 11,264 really stand for 8,000 or 18,000 miles?

The memory is a sort of speedometer and odometer. It tells you how far you have come and how fast you are going. But it is an unreliable device. It remembers some events from long ago and far away, events apparently of no importance. It forgets all sorts of events from more recent times, even those of great importance. Some things it allows to slip to the surface, often at illogical moments. Other things it cannot recognize even when brought to its attention by other people or by letters, diaries, souvenirs.

While the modus operandi of memory remains a mystery, one or two rules are fairly clear. It tends to forget things that are unpleasant and to remember those that are pleasant. It thereby, or simultaneously, lends itself to fondling the ego. Hence, of most of your conversations, you usually remember what you told others and much less of what they told you. That is because what the other person said is just another event like a rainfall or last week's newspaper, whereas what you said has to do with me, me, ME, ME!

The mass media of communication daily bombard us with thousands of experiences and novelties. The memory must forget many things in order to enable the mind to keep up with the sheer stream of events. As a result, people hardly recall last month's sensation or last year's scandal. But when that sensation or scandal impinges directly on their theories and interests, they remember it well and long.

So it is that if you propound the thesis that when supplies are being stolen at the office, it is usually left-handed, red-haired people (or Blacks, Jews, Hispanics, Catholics, Mediterraneans, poor people, or WASPs) who are responsible, your memory will take careful note of every incident of this sort that bears out your thesis and will either ignore or soon forget every incident that contradicts your thesis. The result is that even if the number of red-haired, left-handed people stealing is directly proportional to their numbers among employees, your memory has so handled the situation that your original prejudice against these people is vindicated. Even when the police description based on eyewitnesses' testimony identifies the thief as black-haired and right-handed, you suspect that the culprit wore a wig and tried passing himself off as right-handed or that the police have been bribed or hoodwinked. *We not only perceive what we want to perceive and ignore the rest, but even what we perceive is then subject to further purification by the memory.*

Opinion versus experience

The following examples further demonstrate the ways we distort the truth. Are there some people you do not like and to whom therefore you feel superior? Then you believe the worst about them to be true, and that vindicates your worst suspicions, puts order in your life, and makes you feel better. Let us say that your company hires a woman to be your supervisor, and you are sure that women were not cut out for work in your field or for being chiefs of any sort. No sooner does a snafu take place than you just know that the hiring of the woman was responsible for the mess, whether or not you take the trouble to investigate the incident.

If you know—that is, believe, wish, hope—that Blacks or women are inferior (or equal), that marijuana is harmful (or harmless), that a fetus is (or is not) a living person, you will maintain that opinion in the face of every experience to the contrary. Should conclusive evidence in favor of the opposite position be presented, you dismiss the evidence, the experiment it is based on, the scientists performing the experiment, the agency funding it, the publication describing it.

Mistaken perceptions

What you wish to believe is often what has been instilled in you from childhood on and what you therefore feel comfortable with. Anything that threatens to jolt or change those beliefs creates anxiety, makes it difficult for you to operate by rote, and forces you to think and calculate. It is easy to dismiss that disconcerting information as false. The alternative, of trying to absorb it into your system by rearranging the system to take account of it, is a lot of work that no one likes.

You have written a report for your sociology course or

for your boss at the office. You put a lot of work into it; you were conscientious and resourceful. You hand it in, sure that it is going to get you an A or a promotion. In fact, it comes back with a C or a demotion. What happened? Why are you surprised? Simply because, having made a large investment of time and energy, you could not face the possibility that all of it may have gone to waste. You wished, therefore hoped, *and therefore expected* that the report could garner only good results. You had brought yourself to the point of simply being incapable of entertaining any other outcome. Few are the people who can see their own flaws before others point them out.

REGARDING THE WORLD AS AN EXTENSION OF YOURSELF

You are stepping out with an attractive member of the opposite sex. Things are going along smoothly. You see each other often. You have all kinds of fun together. You both seem to be sliding along to "going steady" or engagement. Then one fine morning, you find out that the beloved is in fact going steady or becoming engaged to someone else. You are startled and destroyed. You cannot believe the information.

The reason is obvious. Your love was so strong that you unconsciously blocked out any contrary signs. Because you wanted to be matched with the beloved, you interpreted all signs in the light of that desire. In order to evade the truth that hurts in the short term, you merely fostered an illusion that led to a greater pain in the long run.

Who has not had the experience of wanting to see or hear something desperately, picking up a newspaper, thinking that it said what you wanted it to say, and discovering that it did no such thing? Or, deeply preoccupied with a certain issue, you walk into the street or into a room and hear conversation. You are surprised that other people, though in no way associated with what preoccupies you, seem to be talking about the matter. Then you discover that, of course, they were not talking about that at all; your own interests had merely caused you to filter the sounds in such a way as to make it seem that even strangers shared your interest.

Not only when you are in love does the whole world seem to be in love, but when you are concerned with anything, the world appears concerned with it too. You have a built-in selfishness that causes you to regard the world as an extension of yourself and to hide the truth about your limited scope.

HAVING OTHERS REINFORCE YOUR IDEAS

Thus it is that you consider as friends those who admire you. You want to have intelligent people for friends, not fools. And people who regard you as intelligent by that very fact prove their own intelligence and deserve respect. The same holds true with love. If a member of the opposite sex falls in love with you, he or she at the least shows a discriminating taste. Sometimes that person may be too unattractive to you for you to reciprocate, but at other times you are at the least impressed and may even respond.

In the same way, you regard as a good conversationalist, not someone who talks well or much, nor someone who excels in lively give–and–take (you tend to regard such people as pushy, wordy, noisy, exhibitionist), but someone who listens carefully to what you say, keeping interruptions and adversary responses to a minimum. Such a person is obviously an excellent talker.

Thus it is often that you read most avidly those newspapers, journals of opinion, and columnists who say the things that you yourself say. You pretend to others and to yourself that you read to obtain information and perspective, but the truth is that you read in good part in order to have your own thoughts reinforced. You want to be soothed and tickled, affirmed and vindicated. You are only incidentally interested, despite all avowals and protestations, in being enlightened, corrected, updated.

You have written a hard-hitting report or story, and you show it to your friend with admonitions to be as candid and critical as possible, that you want the truth, not bromides. Your friend takes you at your word: "The introduction is misleading, the body uneven, the conclusion confusing, the style is flabby, the humor unsuccessful." When he or she returns the piece to you, you are crestfallen, and worse, you allow a cleavage to enter into your relationship. It turns out that you really did not mean what you said. You talked about a critique, but what you expected and wanted was effusiveness, celebration, superlatives.

Illusions fostered by the complicity of others

CANDOR MAY LEAD TO UNHAPPINESS

As if self-delusion were not bad enough, you are deluded as well by others, sometimes because they want to get something out of you but usually because they merely want to remain on good terms with you or are simply polite. Your girl friend buys herself a dress and prides herself on her excellent taste. People have told her that her taste is not all it should be; but she dismisses those remarks by believing that her critics lack taste or that had they seen all her sartorial choices, they would not have been so quick to condemn. But now she has bought a dress and comes to you with the question, "How do you like it?"

In the first place, you are trying to get on with her, and you realize that candor would lead to tension and unhappiness. So you say, "Great!" Even if the person in question were merely a casual acquaintance—not a girl friend—and you had no ulterior motive to lie, you still would not be candid. Why tell the truth and hurt someone's feelings? If she lacks taste, your candor about her latest exhibition of that lapse will not improve her taste. What is the point of hurting someone arbitrarily and for no good reason? It seems sensible to tell a white lie, to keep the conversation on a pleasant level, to part on good terms.

All these are legitimate reasons, but they result in another dash of illusion, another misconception, in the person addressed. *We are not suggesting here that you should be candid and should incur the consequences*; we are merely pointing out the common way of behaving and the consequences of such a way. *Illusion is a product not only of your limitations but also of the complicity of the world around you.* Your illusions are reinforced by the mendacity of people, and concurrently your lies to others sink them deeper into their illusions. No one, no matter how perceptive and alert, is immune to this ailment. Remember Shakespeare's Caesar: He could not be flattered—except by being told that he was beyond flattery, for then he fell, hook, line, and sinker, for the flattery.

Modern society, of which advertising is an important component, is built on flattery and illusion. "Enjoy now, pay later," is the slogan of the modern sensibility, shouted through the bullhorn of media advertising, the theme of numerous commercial interests trying to sell you something. The slogan itself is at once a lie and a form of lying to oneself. It harbors the illusion of enjoyment obtained easily because it has not been paid for yet. Even persons already in a financial hole, who should not commit themselves to activities they cannot afford to pay for now, are sucked into an arrangement that will leave them with ever deeper debts. The normal procedure would be to pay as you go, to enjoy yourself as you earn the money to pay for it. The flattery of advertising, however, lures you into thinking that you can get something for nothing (nothing to be paid *now*) or for little (the individual installment is quite small, especially when compared to what you would have to pay in a pay-as-you-go scheme).

Advertising caters to your illusions in other ways as well. By suggesting that using Brand X hair oil, Brand Y toothpaste, or Brand Z breath freshener will get you that lovely member of the opposite sex that you have long had your eye on, it implies that intelligence, personality, income, style are of little account in social success; whereas the exact reverse is true: *Not your yellowing teeth hamper your social life but your yellowing personality.*

Facing the truth

Part of your problem is not knowing yourself, and that is in turn part of the larger difficulty of knowing anything at all, of your calibrating the perception of things in line with your interests and comforts. Everything would thus seem to conspire to keep you in the ignorance of vanity, self-interest, and comfort.

The solution is to think more clearly, be more open to experiences, be on the lookout for deceptions and especially self-deceptions. Such prescriptions are obviously too general to apply, and instead of trying to achieve a sweeping self-reformation, one would do better to work on it piecemeal.

EXPOSE YOURSELF TO OPPOSING VIEWS

Try, for example, to stop reading only the columnists who reflect your own viewpoint, and expose yourself to others. Try harder to understand these others; the result may be a more open-minded, enlightening outlook.

VERIFY YOUR MEMORIES

Be a little more skeptical of "facts" that seem to reinforce your thesis and less skeptical of those that challenge it. Make a greater effort to verify and validate your perceptions and memories: Write down on a list, if necessary, the times when the pencils were *not* stolen by left-handed, red-haired men. Resort to keeping and periodically reviewing records and diaries so as to correct some of your perceptions and memories.

DON'T JUMP TO HASTY CONCLUSIONS

Refrain, most of all, from jumping too hastily to conclusions. Be *less* sure of yourself and your convictions. *The more sure you are of yourself, the more should you check them out.*

Especially if they pertain to you, they are more than likely to be distorted by you and unreliable.

THINK ABOUT YOUR ASSERTIONS

The next time you get into an argument, think twice about your assertions. Could you be yelling, not because—as you like to think—you are sure of yourself, but rather because you are *un*sure of yourself?—like the legendary preacher who wrote in the margin of his sermon, "Argument weak here. Raise voice."

Let the words of Yeats be a stern warning and inspiration to you:

> The best lack all conviction, while the worst
> Are full of passionate intensity.

7

Punishing
the
Tale Bearer

Ignoring the truth

"Let me know what is bothering you, and I will see what I can do to cure it," says the doctor to the patient, the lawyer to the client. Or as a salesman liked to put it, "Help me to help you." Whatever the line of work, nothing fruitful or important can get done unless there is an accumulation of reliable information, a report on the state of things, a picture of reality.

One would conclude that since mankind wants problems resolved, difficulties eased, questions answered, it is eager to listen to the sources of information, to the bearers of tales, the messengers of the truth. Right? Wrong! Too often people are afraid of the truth or prefer hanging on to some current illusion. And in order to evade reality, they may have to indulge in complicated contortions to make sure that it doesn't impinge on them, disrupting their lives and bland assumptions.

One of these devices is to ignore or even, when possible or necessary, punish the bringer of the news. One can think of many public examples from history and current events of such behavior. But what we reprehend on the part of our political leaders or on the part of the electorate, we practice ourselves in our lives. Here are ways by which we refuse to view events objectively, followed by suggestions on how to face the truth squarely.

THE TEACHER IS "INCOMPETENT"

Say that your child brings home a letter from the teacher that indicates that the child is doing something wrong in class. The reaction of many parents is to grow angry. They then either punish the child or slander the teacher as a bigot or an incompetent. This is done in lieu of sitting down and studying the problem—that is, trying to find out what the child has been doing wrong, asking oneself how one may have contributed to the misbehavior, or more importantly, what one can do now by way of seeing to it that the child will discontinue his or her acting up.

PERSONALIZING COMPLAINTS

Or say that your child raises a complaint directly with you. Most people take such complaints personally. Instead of seeing that he or she is at a stage where children will complain, we personalize it into some response like, "I must be a lousy parent," which—whether or not true—is something hard to alter and causes resentment in ourselves.

Far better would it be to look at the matter objectively, instead of personalizing it, and to say, "I'm doing a bad job just now" or "I'm not following the right course with my child." Such an approach is more helpful, because one's manner of handling a child can easily be changed with a little guidance or introspection.

THEY'RE PICKING ON ANGELIC ME

Or, more commonly perhaps, someone criticizes you at the office. "Smith is always late with his report," Jones says to the boss about you. "You can't depend on him ever to be on time."

Your first reaction is to want to hit the tattletale. The second reaction is to resort to a "you, too": "Yeah, well, I've never seen Jones hand in a report, even if his are always on time, that doesn't have a good dozen typos and smudges on each page. What's the sense of handing in a report on time if no one can read it?"

This is the way many people respond, but it happens to be a rather lame way. The boss, for one thing, rarely swallows the bait. He may not like typos and smudges; but he did not notice that Jones's reports had so many of them, and he thinks either that you're lying outright or innocently exaggerating. In any case, Jones's typos and smudges never did bother him much. Right now he is vexed by your not having your report in on time, not by the appearance of Jones's reports. He therefore regards your remark as a cop-out.

He turns to you and says, "How about that, Smith? How come your reports never are in on time, eh?" You tried to keep the ugly truth about you from coming out by punishing the truth teller, but it didn't work.

So you resort to the fallback device: self-pity. The attack on the tale bearer was a public, open maneuver, and when that didn't work, you slink back psychically into your little cave and you brood there. "They're picking on me!" a comforting little voice whispers. And you soon feel better.

MEET YOUR WORST FRIEND

Do you recognize that voice? Meet the "best" friend you ever had—your other self—"Angelic Me." You know Angelic Me very well, for your version has been with you since you were three or five or seven. That's the one who comes over to you when your mother scolds you, your father punishes you, your cousin lets you have it, or your club ostracizes you.

Then, when you know the loneliest feeling in the world, when you have no one to turn to, no moral reserve to fall back on, you go to your room and cry. Around that time, "Angelic Me" taps you on your shoulder and says to you, "Don't feel bad, chum! You're such a sweet, innocent soul, and they're such a bunch of rotten creeps, every last one of them. Friends, sisters, brothers, or parents—they don't appreciate what a noble, beautiful, gentle soul you have—what a grand person you are.

"All they do is tell terrible stories about how bad you are. But that's all right. Let them carry on the way they do, because basically you don't care, do you? If people can't appreciate you for your greatness—even though you do some bad things once in a while—you don't even want any prizes, love, or attention from such dumb clucks.

"You'll just spend the rest of your life in your room, maybe even in your bed. They'll beg you—in vain—to come out. Or maybe you'll run away from home, and they'll never find you again. Or maybe even you'll just die.

"Boy, will they ever miss you then, all of them! Then

they'll be sorry for the way they treated you and took you for granted and took it out on you. Then they'll know what a beautiful creature you were and how important to their lives. Then they'll wish you were still around; only you won't be."

The history of angelic me

Angelic Me has been around you for a long time. That self, or a variant thereof, hangs around everyone for a while. In some people, that "me" shrivels up during the growing-up period and is rarely heard from after adolescence. In most of us, Angelic Me is a lifetime companion. Though he or she does not, of course, hang around you nearly as much as when you were young, the angelic one does come around at times like these when you're on the carpet.

So when you're criticized on the job or in school, you first try to destroy the critic, no matter how truthful a critic it may be. And then you turn inside and try to relieve yourself with self-pity. It feels so warm and consoling to have Angelic Me hold your hand, to have the halo around your head restored to its proper position after it has been knocked off.

"He's picking on you!" Angelic Me whispers to you now. "They're all—the whole world—against you, willfully misunderstanding you." And then come the rationalizations. "Don't they understand," Angelic Me says, "the problems you face on the job or in school? Don't they see how you try to do a perfect job and that that's why you're late? It's only because you have the term paper retyped until every mistake has been excised that it is late. It's only because they've got you holding down two jobs that it's late."

Kicking the habit

And so you drift out into an ocean of brooding on a current of self-pity. But if you want to change your lifestyle, your passivity, and the world around you, you must stop taking the easy way out. You must dispose of the rationalizations.

YOU DON'T HAVE TO BE A PERFECTIONIST

Sure, you do a perfect job before writing the report, but have you ever asked yourself whether the perfection is wanted or appreciated? Maybe you're doing it so elaborately merely in order to satisfy something in yourself. There is no one out there who would notice the difference between a perfect and a merely competent report. The company or your professor probably does not consider the extra time necessary for perfection as worth the effort involved. Maybe the constant retyping for perfection is unnecessary. Instead of vainly trying to change others according to the dictates of your demanding conscience, you might entertain the idea that this company, or this instructor, is more interested in the substance of the report than in the format, more interested in meeting deadlines than in outlawing smudges and typos.

Or if the extra time and the perfection are necessary, perhaps you should therefore start on your report earlier. Instead of postponing it and killing time, as you usually do, until there are only a few days left, and then trying to get everything done in the limited time, pace yourself. If perfection really is your goal, you should apportion your time accordingly.

ANALYZE YOUR ERRORS

When you apply this sort of analysis to yourself, the lament, "He's picking on me," turns out to mean only, "I may be too lazy, defeatist, passive, confused to do something constructive about my problem." It means basically, "I'm picking on myself."

Rather than rationalize your inadequacies, you should analyze your error. Instead of trying to silence the truth teller, you should try to cease your self-destructive behavior. Instead of withdrawing to your psychic cell and pitying yourself, you should change that self. *Some things you cannot change in others or in the world around you, but you can change in yourself. That change will in turn affect the world around you and its attitudes toward you.*

OTHERS MAY BE ABLE TO SEE YOU BETTER
THAN YOU SEE YOURSELF

To effect those changes, you must begin listening to what others—Dr. Jones your teacher, Rollins the boss, Sheila your girl friend, Marilyn your sister, Perkins your enemy—are saying to you and about you. The people with whom one surrounds oneself are, among other things, mirrors. They emit signals, and you'd better make your antennae more receptive. Buried within exaggerations, distortions, and misconceptions in their statements are to be found kernels of truth about you. Stop punishing and start listening to these messengers and tale bearers.

FIRE ANGELIC ME AND HIRE MATURE ME

Above all, you should have it out with Angelic Me, who has for so long been your private advisor, Prime

Minister, Secretary of State, and Chief of Staff in your war with reality. That "me" is, really, a traitor in your psyche. Instead of personalizing issues by attacking others, you should confront yourself by firing Angelic Me. Start listening to the others and stop listening to this specter. For too long, Angelic Me has been working against you under the guise of working for you. For too long has this ghost been your worst enemy while pretending to be your best friend. For too long has such a phony been allowed to besmirch the truth tellers while lying to you left and right. For too long, in short, have you allowed yourself to be the victim of an impersonation, a grand hoax: The creature called Angelic Me is actually Devilish Me, Peevish Me. That is, *Childish Me*.

Accepting Differences

LET'S ALL SING TOGETHER—OR ELSE!

Once you have excised "Angelic Me," you have regained the strength and maturity to be *You* and let others be *Themselves*. You are now ready to face someone else. For there is another kind of tale bearer who brings out the worst in us. That is the person who differs from us and therefore is, or seems to be, a slur on our own values. We all know that moment in summer camp or at a Scout cookout when an entertainment counselor says, "All right, now. Let's all sing together!" And everyone jumps into the song jamboree. Pure innocent fun, right? Yet in a way, that incident symbolizes some not so innocent tendencies.

At that songfest, everyone pitches in, because even if they cannot carry a tune, they enjoy making believe they can. Even those not crazy about singing enjoy at least the company and the communal horseplay. And if they do not sing, no one harasses them or considers them inferior or traitors. Yet the whole of human history can be read as a gigantic series of songfests at which various leaders have said, "Let's All Sing Together!" and have then proceeded to burn at the stake, crucify, or torture those who preferred not to.

For not only is the urge to conform strong in us, but equally strong is the urge to make others conform. It is as if people say to themselves, If the dissidents can get away with doing their own thing instead of joining the chorus, then why am I joining when I am free not to do so too? Am I therefore shown up as lazy or insecure? And if they can, so can others, and soon there will be no songfest.

Here is a cause of prejudice and intolerance directed at those with differing religious, political, or moral beliefs. It is, you say, political and remote from me and my problems of coping? Yes and no. Remote it may be, but also relevant. Don't many people, in their circle, social club, or at work and school, operate in this fashion? We all need, as we saw, a whipping boy, and usually appoint the truth teller to that role. *For the truth tellers, the tale bearers are the ones who will not sing along but listen to their own inner music.*

MARCHING TO A DIFFERENT DRUMMER

The whipping boy does not have to suffer the extremities of the concentration camp or the bonfire. More "civilized" weapons are at hand for use by some people. Anyone who does not sing together with us, we consider not so much subversive or wicked as mad. And that madness is proved by the person's not singing with us. Anyone we do not understand—that is, who does not make sense—clearly is mad.

Look at Russia. Those who deny that they are living in a communist worker's paradise are placed in an lunatic asylum. Insofar as sanity and madness are dependent on the sense of the majority of the people, the action is not entirely illogical. The few are clearly out of step with the majority, and that is a fair definition of madness.

We often use the word *mad* about other people. Obviously, who is mad and who is not matters greatly. Virtually all of us set ourselves up as experts on, and models of, sanity. From this vantage point, you can condemn as "mad" all those who differ with you, who happen not to sing along in whatever chorus you are into at the moment. Very convenient. If you are a Hottentot in religion or a Zilch in politics, you fraternize mainly with fellow Hottentots or Zilchers and consider all other people in the community, especially lapsed Hottentots or Zilchers, as having a screw loose upstairs—out of contact with reality, unaware of the facts, living by fantasies, myths, lies. To make such a statement about others is to imply that you—and all those in your chorus singing along—are in contact with reality and are aware of the facts.

The individual who represents some dissenting minority view in a community, who refuses to sing along, thereby calls into question the prevailing wisdom and disconcerts those singing. As long as everyone is singing together, the definitiveness of the truth they celebrate is clear-cut. But to have a nonsinger, or someone singing in a different key, marching to a different drummer, raises the question of whether the obvious and widely held truth is the truth at all. For if it is the truth, how can anyone not accede to it?

Two explanations are then possible. One is that the dissenter is right and the singing majority is wrong. The other is that the solitary, by decrying the obvious, is a self-evident nut and that the sing-along crowd is as righteous and just as ever. Obviously, the latter explanation, the more satisfactory one to the singing majority, is the one adopted. But, alas, the judgment of history is that many individuals now worshipped as great were the annoying tale bearers to the society and dismissed the conventional reading of reality. When Galileo insisted that the earth revolves around the sun, when Columbus insisted that the world was round, they were dismissed as madmen by people unable to understand why they would not sing along.

AVOID THE CROWD'S SNAP JUDGMENT

Beware, then, of falling in with the crowd's snap judgments and gut reactions. Look into the matter on your own. Don't take the common view for granted; don't assume that the nonsinger, the tale bearer, the marcher to a different drummer, is wrong. If others choose to be simple-minded, that is their privilege, but don't you be that way. Reacting against the tale bearer and nonsinger is one of the ways people have of dodging reality, limiting their perceptions, making self-knowledge difficult, and throwing obstacles in the way of coping.

8
Taking Things for Granted

Knowing oneself and knowing reality are problematic because of the difficulties inherent in the process of finding out anything. Most people assume that reality is out there and is readily perceived and assimilated. Any problems about that are of the philosopher's making, and philosophers certainly spend a lot of time and words ruminating over what and how we know. Yet if it was only a matter for specialized study, one would be inclined to leave it at that; but the question has great import for simple problem solving in everyday life.

The way you act is based on what you think you know. Any change in what you know and in how you think you know is bound to affect your sense of yourself and others and your interactions with people. Most people, though, never look at themselves or their thought processes. Hence any lessons in coping and attempted self-regeneration must take account of the process.

Two hurdles confront the person trying to separate true from false in the mind. One is external—the difficulty of obtaining information correctly from the world around us, specifically from other people. The other is internal— the necessary habit of taking things for granted.

GETTING THE MESSAGE SNARLED

It is a well-known fact about human nature that it garbles even simple messages, that it cannot understand things and pass them on with clarity. This has tremendous implications. It means that you cannot pride yourself on your prowess, because you yourself cannot be relied on to pass messages along to others any more than anyone else can to you. You may think, as we saw in Chapter 2, that you are exempt from the human condition and are, unlike all those other people, more reliable and trustworthy. But you are just as prone to making mistakes as anyone else.

An important implication is that *insofar as most of what you know is derived from what others tell you or write down in books, magazines, and newspapers on the basis of what others tell them, there are many uncertainties in what you know.* This too should make you a little less assertive and more humble in your espousal of any position.

HOW SURE CAN YOU BE?

You may have a problem relating to other people because of your insistence that what you happen to believe in is the truth and that all other ideas and versions are incorrect. You never can understand how people persist in their erroneous beliefs; their devotion to Catholicism, Protestantism, Judaism, or Atheism; Conservatism or

Liberalism; Capitalism or Socialism; Baseball or Football. Not content with merely presenting your outlook, you have to try to force others to stop believing their nonsense. You have to shout, and when they won't yield, you resort to personal attacks: "You're a radical only because you never liked your father, and that is how you are getting back at him!" You end up making yourself disliked by everyone.

The point to remember is that not only should you not see red when the other person disagrees with you, even if you are right and he or she is wrong, but that you may not even be right. Sure, you are solidly wedded to your position, but can you be so certain that it is the right one? How do you know?

Does not that "knowledge"—which is really belief, opinion, even conjecture—rest on hearsay evidence, on what people told you or told each other and then wrote down? How do you know that capitalism really does, or does not, work? Or the same about communism? The evidence either way is strong—that is, contradictory. The fact that most people, especially the ones you look up to and get your information from, loudly assert one or the other position does not prove a thing, except that *they may be as deluded as you are*. The question, "How do you know what you know?" applies as strongly to them as to you.

Taking things for granted

THE ASSUMPTION

The simple fact is that *all knowledge rests on assumptions*. Any statement anyone makes, even every word in the statement, rests on various assumptions. Many are trivial, some are important; every statement or set of statements has at least one important assumption.

An assumption is a belief that is accepted as true without evidence or proof. If, despite the absence of proof, faith in assumptions did not exist, no statement would be possible, because any attempt to prove something consists of statements that of necessity rest on assumptions. Normally we have good reasons for accepting the belief without challenge. But every once in a while, someone does challenge it, and then we discover that the assumption was not valid.

Thus if you say, "Socrates is a smart man," you assume that Socrates is a human being and is to be judged accordingly as smart or dumb; you do not assume that Socrates is an angel, divinity, or beast. In this case, the assumption is a fair one; everyone assents to it. But if you say, "The skyrocketing cost of gasoline is ruining American life," you assume that increased gasoline prices are in themselves bad; that is, you do not bother to prove it, because you think everyone accepts that as self-evident.

But in point of fact, various people—including dignitaries like presidents and congressmen—think that insofar as high gasoline prices will force people to grow less dependent on the automobile and more dependent on public transport, society can only benefit from the consequent reduction in air pollution, traffic jams, highway accident rates. Thus you have accepted something to be true that really is not.

Most assertions are more like this arguable sort than they are like the one on Socrates. In fact, the more sensitive the topic, the more likely the statements are to rest on questionable assumptions. *And the quarrel between you and your opponent turns on your opponent's making assumptions different from yours*—that is, on matters in good part beyond proof and persuasion.

The philosopher is equal to the garbage collector

The important thing about assumptions is that they are equal in weight or that, like death, they are equalizers. Many assumptions are a matter of definition or of taste; and just as one person prefers coffee and another tea—without logical reason—so one individual makes one assumption about reality, another makes an entirely different one. All people are entitled to assumptions of their own choosing. The philosopher's assumptions are not superior to the garbage collector's, even though for amount and authoritativeness of evidence, cogency and consistency of reasoning, articulateness and eloquence of presentation, the philosopher leaves the garbage collector far behind. The philosopher can evolve a much more impressive thesis than the garbage collector can, but the assumptions it rests on will be no more impressive.

A chain of uncertainties

Professional Opinion

Assumptions bear on all sorts of simple daily judgments. When friends and relatives recommend a particular doctor, you quickly notice the shallowness of the reasoning: I had this problem, and it went away. But how do you know that the doctor had anything to do with it? Perhaps it was the placebo effect: The mere act of consulting professional opinion and taking a medicine (*any* medicine) made you feel better. Perhaps it was the course of nature: If you had not consulted a physician, the ailment would have left anyway, possibly even more quickly than was the case. Perhaps it was an easy task: Another doctor would have disposed of this ailment just as speedily,

91

only with less show business and at smaller expense. Just as all assertions rest on assumptions, which in turn rest on assumptions, and so on to infinity—so do someone's recommendations of an expert rest on a chain of uncertainties.

Assumptions also bear on our anger, guilt feelings, and values.

ANGER

It takes considerable temerity for anyone to be entirely sure that his or her view of God, of the political order, of the economic system, or of the proper morality is the correct one. The next time you get into one of these discussions, remember that *your argument is only as strong as your assumptions*, which are not very strong at all.

Why are you therefore so determined in your thinking? That your opponents are fanatical is no excuse; that merely shows *their* ignorance of the fragility of their argument, with its dependence on vulnerable assumptions.

How sure can you be?

Part of the problem may be your temper, which has its roots in psychological causes. But insofar as your temper is kindled by only certain issues, you should leave these alone. As the old Victorian adage had it, no gentleman discusses religion, politics, or sex in polite company. As a universal maxim, this is unacceptable; but for some people, it is excellent advice. If you cannot discuss religion, politics, or morality without getting into a shouting match or questioning the patriotism, integrity, or decency of people disagreeing with you, you had better stick to nonflammable topics.

Don't blow your stack just because someone does not share your assumptions—because they read reality differently than you do. One person's guess about the truth is as good as another's. If you can't approach such discussions in a spirit of joint exploration or fun, the way one plays basketball or chess with friends—not to win at any cost but to exercise muscles and have a good time—then forget about it, and leave civilized discourse to other people.

ASSUMPTIONS AND GUILT

The discovery of the prominence of assumptions bears also upon the arguments you have within yourself, upon your guilt feelings. Here the corrective is to apply to yourself the questioning process used by, among others, philosophers and therapists. You must question the reason for those actions and beliefs that cause you difficulties until you have worked your way back to some irrational and expendable starting point. Every action and every belief rests on some other belief, and the arguments used on behalf of that belief contain, besides good reasoning and acceptable evidence, at least a few dubious assumptions. If one's mind, as are most people's, is stuffed with shallow and superstitious ideas picked up from all sorts of unreliable sources—unthinking individuals, books of fantasy and myth—one is going to suffer. *The weight of the past, which sometimes carries nuggets of wisdom but usually consists of tons of dross, comes down particularly hard on those acting with assurance upon unexamined assumptions about the nature of reality.* Most of the world's suffering is caused by widespread ignorance and gullibility, by inability or unwillingness to isolate and examine premises.

VALUES

Your values and assumptions must always be reexamined to keep up with changing times, ways of thought, ideas. Some people mock such keeping up with the times as merely being fashionable, and in a way it is. Neckties wide one year and narrow another year is a matter of fashion, not of broadening horizons. But some new ideas, such as doing away with slavery, implementing women's rights, limiting the length of the workday, are changes for the better and are part of the general march toward the realization of certain ideals, the discarding of superstitions and repressive customs, the growth of compassion for other human beings. Such good changes should be going on inside you just as in the society at large.

Take education. Until recently, in many families, not going to college was regarded with horror. Not to be a college graduate meant exclusion from the middle class. In families wedded to this thinking, the decision by a son or daughter not to seek higher education was seen as a rejection of parental sacrifices and values.

But college is not for everyone. If you enjoy working with your hands and are good at it, follow your interests. You may have to go to a technical school to develop your skills, but you will be doing what you are good at. Your family's values do not have to determine your present and future. Especially if these values are not in line with your own best interests, there is no need to feel guilty about it.

Or there is the example of taking a semester or a year off from school. Traditionally, you finished college in four years. Still, dropping out of school may prove beneficial to you if you use the time to pursue other interests. This action doesn't mean that you will not return to school. It means, rather, that four consecutive years of university schooling may not be the best way for you to benefit from college.

Love and marriage

Unexamined assumptions are as common in personal decisions as in vocational ones. A young couple falling in love may not realize the responsibilities and burdens that will flow out of their current bliss. Having two mortgages and three cars, four children and two jobs, is surely not what most people set out to obtain. *It is rather what they ended up with as a result of going from one step to the next without considering the importance of their actions.*

Though most would agree that a life of sex without love is, except to the Don Juan personality, insufficiently fulfilling, does it follow that a love affair must lead into marriage? If people marry because they fear that without that piece of paper their relationship will be so vulnerable that the slightest pull will rip it apart, they must ask themselves if that relationship is worth keeping in the first place.

YOU MUST DECIDE WHO YOU ARE
BEFORE YOU DECIDE WHAT YOU WANT

The point then is not that love, marriage, and children are bad, but that not everyone is cut out for any or all of these things. They are different things to different people, and you must find out *who* you are before you decide *what* you want from life. *The usual way—of accumulating things and responsibilities and expecting one's identity and goals to be clarified thereafter—is fraught with danger.* One may discover, as more and more couples are doing nowadays, that though one likes children, one does not like them enough to put up with a cramped life-style.

Nothing said so far is to be taken as antilove, antimarriage, antichildren. The point is, again, that not everyone is cut out for any or all of these things. Society, religion, and parents tend to impose on young people venerable values and conventional norms. But each person must alone ascertain what exactly his or her own tastes, capacities, and strengths are. No one can do that for you, not even your parents. To let others dictate one's choices in these basic matters, which so highly affect one's life, is to abdicate responsibility, lack individuality, and solicit entrapment.

The values are yours and yours only. The consequences of your decision will be yours and yours only. Make sure, therefore, that the decision you make is yours and yours only. All regeneration involves thinking afresh, and such thinking requires questioning of assumptions. All problems of coping are ultimately problems in assumptions—which to reject and which to adopt or retain.

When Hamlet says, "Nothing is good or bad but thinking makes it so," he spoke of assumptions. Whether the glass is half full or half empty is a matter of perspective. Pessimists like to look at it as half empty. By questioning your assumptions, however, you can be turned into the optimist, who sees it rather as half full.

9

What You Believe Depends on Where You're At

The generation gap

Whereas facts and logic are universally applicable and acceptable, assumptions by contrast are a matter of individual experience and perspective. They are at the heart of individuality—and of conflicts.

"Bah!" blurts out your grandfather. "This younger generation is gutless and lazy. If they really tried hard, they would get jobs. I did."

It is useless to tell him that he was young and making it in the 1920s, years of seemingly boundless opportunity and prosperity, and that this is the 1970s, years of shrinking opportunity, depletion of resources, and high unemployment.

"Bah!" he blurts out at another time. "Finish high school? College? What do they need that nonsense for? *I* didn't go to high school or college, and I did fairly well. *I* went to the University of Hard Knocks."

It is equally useless to inform him that in the 1920s, few people went to college, and college degrees were required of only a small number of people for a small number of jobs; whereas in the 1970s, a good education—whether in college or a training school—is required for almost all jobs.

His outburst is typical, not—as we like to think—of grandfather's generation, but of all grandparents in any period. They see reality in terms set by their perceptions and responses during their youth, and they continue to see it that way even after they grow old and the reality has changed considerably. The trouble is not that the generation that matured in the 1920s is peculiarly benighted and the generation that matured in the 1970s is unusually enlightened, but that grandparents always live in another world, the world of their youth. So will it also happen to the current young generation. In the 2020s, when it reaches an impressive age and wisdom, it will think and talk in terms appropriate to the 1970s.

The perpetual quarrel of youth and age—as real as that between male and female, black and white, rich and poor—is itself symptomatic of another difficulty in the apprehension of the truth: For most people, the truth, the perception of reality, is determined by their immediate circumstances. With the possible exception of philosophers and seers, *what you see is contingent on where you see it from.*

See the world from your own perspective

This means, among other things, that you can rely on no one else to counsel you, because no one else is in quite your condition and sees things from your perspective, knows precisely where the shoe pinches and how hard the pain is. You must stop looking to others for answers to the riddles of your life, for ways of coping with your problems. Like too many supposedly "selfish" people, you lead a life of errant selflessness in the sense that you are involved in a hopeless rat race of competitiveness, conformity, and other-directedness. True selfishness would have you look to your own needs and circumstances. Here are some ways in which you make yourself feel inadequate by adopting others' frames of reference instead of your own.

You and your job

It is silly to compare your financial position and your place in the pecking order with just any and all other people. You have to take into account your potential and your starting point. Given the economic background you come from, the education you have had, the physical limitations you may have, and the untapped potential you may still make use of, you have to ask yourself how far have you gone? You might discover that, unhappy though you are with your condition, it is perhaps the best available under the present circumstances.

In short, are you taking constructive steps? In lieu of self-rebuke and brooding, you should analyze where things went wrong and see if adjustments can be made accordingly. Remember, these are only present circumstances. Nothing is final.

Is it lack of education and training that is holding you back? Almost every community has an adult education center or junior college. Visit it, look over the course catalogue, make an appointment with the school's coun-

selor to discuss your career objectives. You do not have to
keep your present job for the rest of your life if it is making you unhappy. Remember, at birth you weren't programmed to be a gas station attendant, salesperson,
teacher, or accountant. Although people differ in abilities,
personality, and interests, every person's makeup has the
requisites for success in many occupations.

YOU AND YOUR RELIGION

Because of the dependence of an idea on its circumstances, even the best-intentioned people can sometimes
make you feel inadequate unfairly. Take the case of the
person or group that would have you feel guilty for not
being religious. No doubt, for someone raised in a religious environment and with emotions formed by experiences having to do with ecclesiastical institutions, religion
will forever contain associations of warmth, familiarity,
community. Such people, should they break away, will feel
lost.

Religion also has many useful roles to play in the individual's everyday life, no less than in the society at large. It
provides answers to enigmatic questions. It endows the
universe with a purpose and system, with justice and
poetry. Without it, life would seem meaningless, absurd,
and dull to many people whose work, personal lives, or
health is flawed. Religion can be a vital force, enabling one
to cope and to live life with a decent amount of hope, happiness, and productivity. If your life has been lax, easygo-
ing, unstructured, you probably need a bit of discipline
and structure in it.

The Procrustean bed

What one must beware of, however, is the Procrustean bed—fitting everyone to the same bed and stretching

out by force those who are too short and cutting off the feet of those too long. To insist that religion is the answer for every individual and to every problem is to act, or react, rigidly, mindlessly. You must determine where you stand on religion and then ignore the pressures from the other camp to become like them. You must go your own way according to your own needs and rules, your experiences and judgments, and not according to any externally imposed ones. You must first find yourself, and finding yourself in turn means coming to terms with religion.

Living up to the dictates of one's mind becomes difficult when religion is in play. How often do people rebuke themselves as terrible sinners, make double vows to reform, assure themselves that this time they mean it and that next week they really will live up to their religion—only then to flunk once again? What we suggest is that *the failure rate may be due to a basic disbelief in the religion.* A true believer would not have this much difficulty "going straight." What you may have is the *dry, hollow shell of practice and the missing kernel of belief.* The moral system and practice have—out of habit—survived the atrophy of belief, hence the difficulty of making the body conform to the will.

What will work

Wise men will opt neither for nor against religion, but for what will work. If you can revive your faith and live at one with yourself, more power to you! But if you cannot do that, you should dispose of the religious nagging. Our suggestion is that if you cannot achieve a resurgence of the old faith, try the alternative: not to revive the faith, but to send out after it the moral system that was a part of it. You may find that to be the easier and more meaningful way.

Our concern is with putting you in harmony with yourself, with unity of being; and we would have you follow the line of least resistance rather than harassing yourself over impossibilities and giving yourself pointless suffering.

If, in short, you are on good terms with God, then religion and its rigidities are not the causes of your problems. To a semi- or nonreligious person, such things as sexual continence are frustrating and painful. To a religious person, however, any discomfort caused by restraints is eclipsed by the happiness of knowing that for a little pain in this world, one stores up an eternity of bliss. Such people take downright delight in their physical deprivations—medieval monks went out of their way to perform what they called "mortification of the flesh"—knowing that the bottom line is joy forever. Such people are at ease with themselves.

However, people who are not sure of their beliefs, of the afterworld, of the purpose of continence, are caught between two worlds; and their anxiety is due to their inability to tell to which they belong. Such people might well relish religion and its consolations—*if* they can.

The Sunset Law

If you find that you cannot, then consider this option: Clear your mind of the relics of a faith you no longer have. Free yourself of restrictions, the rationale of which makes no sense to you. Unburden yourself of rules and ideas that are no longer a part of you as they once were part of the child you were and of the parents and teachers who imposed them on you. *If, upon mature reflection, these values make sense, go for them. But to persist in adhering to values unexamined for decades is foolish.*

The French Revolution, historians say, was caused when the structure of political power no longer reflected the power groupings in the realm, when those who ruled lacked money, clout, and popular backing. In the same way do many people move from one set of values to another without that change being registered in their life-styles. Their impulses reflect their new, adult ways but are held back by the rules and restrictions imposed during the callow, childish days. Their minds are a hodgepodge of current and useful, as well as of archaic and useless, ideas. Such people are like the Englishman who, migrating from a region where it rains virtually every day, continues, in Southern California or New Mexico, where it rarely rains, to go to work with his furled umbrella on his arm. Or like the woman who grew up in poverty and upon becoming prosperous still wears out her clothes as if each dress were the only one she had, as was the case in her youth. Such a person should sit down, think the matter through, and see that she can let herself go for doom is not around the corner.

There is a movement afoot to pass a Sunset Law, whereby every government program is not automatically renewed but would have to be rejustified from scratch. Whether government should be run in this fashion is a matter of your politics, but the individual's psyche *has* to be run in this way. *Go whichever way you want, but do so only after reflection and self-examination, not out of habit and blindness.* As part of the Sunset Law of your psyche, periodically review your values, commitments, and life-styles to see if and where they have ceased being in tune with yourself and with current facts. How foolish to adhere to concepts that are based on values that no longer have your allegiance. Either go back to the religion, or get rid of these concepts, and replace them with those reflective of your current outlook.

THE LIBERAL CITY SLICKER

The interplay of truth and circumstance can also be seen in the sociological field. Take the liberal-minded person who declares proudly that he, for one, is not joining the general flight from city to suburb. He believes that the city has a future and that every urbanite is obliged to make a stand there, for if such people leave, who will be left except the very rich and the very poor?

The decision to stay in the city is commendable, but the tone of self-righteousness, with its implied rebuke to you who have joined the unseemly flight, is not. What is unmentioned but crucial is that he, liberal though he may be, also happens to have the money that enables him to send his children to private school and thereby circumvent the problematic city public schools. Indeed, his money serves in general to insulate him from many of the ills and deficiencies of the city; whereas you, not having the money, are not so insulated and cannot avail yourself of private school. The view of the stage from the tenth row, center aisle, is not the same as from the last rows in the side gallery.

Psyching out

People spouting high ideals can make the unwary uncomfortable. Those so speaking may not realize the discomfort they are causing, although some may be fully or partly aware and are indulging in psyching out. You will feel morally inferior and guilty unless you keep your wits about you long enough to make some elementary distinctions about circumstances and opportunities.

Morality is, after all, a luxury. You have to have money to be able to elevate yourself above the grind of survival, to give to charity. The high ideals spouted by some people, conservative no less than liberal, sound good in the abstract but are not universally applicable. That everyone should work for their money and not get handouts from the state is, as conservatives often proclaim, a noble principle. The only trouble is that the person proclaiming the principle has a good job or a comfortable business—perhaps even one obtained through inheritance. He or she may be unaware of how other people not so fortunately established in life are unable to get any job at all. It is easy for others to urge you to be more independent—or liberal—when they have the wherewithal to do so and you do not. Once you realize this fact, you will not feel inadequate over your nonheroic stance.

WHOM ARE YOU COMPARING YOURSELF WITH?

You can only overcome this type of one-upmanship by thinking clearly and taking stock of yourself. What is the use of comparing yourself with someone more successful? Have you had a comparable head start—that is, education, financial help from parents, physical endowment? If you must compare yourself—and sometimes it is useful to do so in order to get a sense of one's achievements—you should look to people you knew and grew up with. What are they up to, and how are they doing?

Getting unstuck

If you find yourself coming out behind in such comparisons, it is time to ask yourself other questions. How many options have you allowed to lapse? How many talents squandered? Are any of them recoverable? If it is possible to change jobs, the fault may be yours. Is it laziness? Incompetence? What are the odds of breaking out? Of course, certain options may not be available to you right now. You may be too young or too old at present, or you may lack proper training.

Being "stuck" is a matter of viewpoint. If you see that no alternatives are possible, you resign yourself more easily than when you tell yourself you could or should have done something else. Being "stuck" means that you will not look for new opportunities. The first thing to do therefore is to "unstick" your thinking. Being "unstuck" means that you are able to investigate new opportunities and realize that change in yourself is possible.

Everything is relative

Your problem may be that you brood over your supposedly low position. Yet everyone is a failure in comparison with someone else. Being a monarch certainly sounds like a wonderful condition to be born into, but being, say, Queen of Holland is small potatoes compared to being Queen of Great Britain. And the latter no doubt feels inferior in power and range of options to her namesake, Elizabeth I. The latter, in turn, felt hemmed in compared to her father Henry VIII, and so on down the line.

No one believes that he is where the action is, that he or she has all the power and freedom he could use. A character in Shakespeare remarks that you never reach bottom; no matter how bad off you think you are, you can always find some other person who is even worse off than you. You need not feel stepped on, as though you were the only person in the world who has problems.

A student was complaining about conditions in school—the boredom, the humiliation, the meaningless work, the virtual morons one had to associate with. A friend listened patiently to the list of complaints in order to compare it to his own experience and then inquired if the complainer was required to take a foreign language.

"Foreign language? No, my school has no such requirement."

"What about calculus?"

"Same thing."

"Weekly quizzes?"

"No, we're too busy to be bothered with things like that."

"Midterms?"

"Our school does not do that sort of thing."

"My God!" his friend interjected. "And you're complaining about your school! You don't have to put up with one-tenth of the requirements and Mickey-Mouse work that I do or that 95 percent of the students did and do."

The poor fellow had lived a privileged existence and because of his constant tendency to gripe, never even had the sense to know it and enjoy it. Are you like him?—so busy feeling sorry for yourself and lamenting to all who will listen about how victimized you are, when in fact you may well be blessed—compared to other people?

Living within your means and for yourself

And just as all individuals feel themselves failures compared to everyone else, so are all people failures compared to their own goals. As a result of advertising, you often find yourself saying, How come *I* don't fly for a week to Monte Carlo or Acapulco? It must be me who is out of step. The answer is that you are in step with yourself, listening to yourself, marching to your own drummer—if only you knew it. You may be making yourself unhappy by thinking you are out of step. Despite the insinuation of the ads, those who do things like flying to Monte Carlo or Acapulco for a week are a distinct and privileged minority, and you likely will never be like them (unless you should win the million-dollar lottery). You think you should live like them, because the impression is created by the media that nearly everybody does. That is clearly not so.

Don't let the media image bother you. It has nothing to do with reality. Just a helpful reminder: When J. Paul Getty—one of the wealthiest men in the world—died a few years ago, a long article in the newspaper revealed the curious information that he loved California best of all the states in America but that he had not been there in the last twenty-five years of his life. Why not? He was too busy!

So it is not only you who cannot get to go where you want to go; you are in the company of some very special people. If J. Paul Getty could not find the time to get to where he wanted to go for reasons of business, his life-style—despite the several billions that separated him from you—was not really so different from that of someone like yourself.

Not that having money is a guarantee against boredom, restlessness, aspirations. A man like Nelson Rockefeller was politically ambitious and wanted to be governor and president. Why did he not just take his money and enjoy it in retirement? Because money is a great need only to those who have not got it. Those who do have it find themselves needing, like Rockefeller, something else.

Your beliefs and desires depend on where you're at

Everything is alluring to somebody, but nothing—not even money—seems to content anyone for long. How, then, can things be at the same time attractive and unattractive? What you believe, and desire, depends on where you're at. So take it easy; your desires are neither absolute nor permanent. Tomorrow you may find yourself in a position totally opposite where you are today. No wonder your face in the mirror keeps on saying to you, "*If you only knew!*"

The Hurdles in the Head

Two things have been established so far: that many notions you have of yourself—your alleged inferiority, superiority, solitude, communion with others, maturity—are misconceptions, and that they are caused by the universal inability of human beings to perceive, listen to, and remember the truth or to obtain a foolproof starting point for deliberations on the truth. These two problems, however theoretical, philosophical, or psychological they may seem, bear directly on your inability to cope and your dissatisfaction with the way your life is going. Not knowing the truth means being out of contact with reality; it means potential disaster—rather as a man driving in a thick fog does not know that an upcoming curve in the road is going to make a startling impact on his consciousness.

Now that we have cleared away the theoretical groundwork, we can focus more completely on the task of self-improvement and regeneration. This task involves clarification of certain fundamentals of behavior.

111

For one thing, motives are an important part of the essential
you. Bringing to bear on them too high expectations is to doom
oneself to fruitless navel-contemplation and frustration. You can
live relatively contented when you learn to live with your own
feelings—that is, to accept the idea that your "motive" is always a
mosaic of instincts, wishes, fears, ambivalences.

One motive in particular needs scrutiny. Envy is an emotion
nearly everyone entertains and must learn to put to constructive
uses and not, as moralists would have it, to squelch—which is an
impossible feat, in any case. Envy is pernicious only when it involves you in trying to emulate others on their ground rather than
in finding your own niche.

Since defeat and frustration are common occurrences to most
people because of the seductiveness and accessibility of pipe
dreams, the way in which you come to terms with defeat can spell
the difference between your bouncing back and going on to new
challenges or your lapsing into passivity, exhaustion, paralysis.

Moreover, language is the medium of conversation, instruc-
tion, thought, and therefore knowledge. It must be made to work
for you and not to work on you, for people are easily confused
and manipulated by mere words. One result of such errancy is entrapment in a vicious cycle, the inability or unwillingness to exercise free choice among the commitments to be made at various
stages of one's growth and development. Another lamentable result
is the compulsion to unquestioningly accumulate things, possessions, and gadgets, even at the cost of having to work hard and
long.

Behind many of these difficulties lurks the greatest hurdle,
that set up by the worst of all tyrants, King Habit. If you can but
revolt and overthrow him, you will confront nothing less than life
itself—raw, naked, unshaped, challenging, even scary, but also
rich.

10

Learning
to Live
with Your Feelings

Motives are always mixed

The difficulty of ascertaining the truth applies not only to the external objective world but all the more so to the nebulous interior world of motives and feelings. For here we enter a murky realm indeed.

An account executive in an advertising agency takes a position on a certain issue facing the company. Invariably, one hears—especially if it is near promotion time—that he has an ulterior motive—he wants to get promoted. Even those people who do not accept the charge find themselves somewhat suspicious of the account executive. Others, especially if they share their views with the critics rather than with the account executive, think that an important point has been made, an insight offered.

The truth, however, is nothing so exciting or novel; *everyone's* motives are mixed. One might as well be told that

the account executive eats three meals a day as that his
motives are mixed with reference to a particular matter.
To understand what we are saying, try this exercise
on yourself. You went or are going to college. Why? To obtain a degree, which is necessary for a job? To improve
your social life by greatly increasing the number of en-
counters with members of the opposite sex? To initiate a
career in professional athletics by first developing your talents and making your mark on a college team? To establish
numerous contacts for future careers in one of the professions or in politics? To dodge work for four more years
and to have a good time? Or to obtain an education, irres-
pective of whether you get the degree or not?

The point is not only that each person goes to college
for a different reason but also that many people go for
more than one reason. Many want some sort of liberalizing
education, but they also want that modern union card, a
degree. They certainly hope to improve their social life,
and they are not averse to making contacts for the future,
having a good time along the way, and participating in one
or several sports.

Once one accepts this reality, one can learn to live
with multiplicity and doubt. All people have numerous—mixed—motives for anything they undertake. The
question, then, becomes not about the state of the individual's motives but about: (1) the circumstances in which
we judge people and their motives, and (2) the relation of
their words to their actions.

Were the account executive up before the holy judgment seat, the state of his motives would be important, because in Christianity doing the right thing is not as important as doing it for the right reason. But in more homely
circumstances, such as being promoted at the ad agency or

running for political office, motives can hardly be as important as actions. People who complain that a politician's stand is motivated by the desire to get elected forget that politicians are always eyeing the next election. That is, after all, what the very word "politician" means in a democracy—someone who tries to get and stay elected. Anyone failing at the task is only an ex-politician.

ISSUES OR MOTIVES?

At issue rather is this: Does the man's stand contradict everything he stood for before? Does he have a habit of taking stands at election (or promotion) time and then ignoring them? Does he follow through on his words this time? Or does he seem equivocal in taking the stand? These are the criteria to be brought to bear: whether his position is credible, not what his major or ultimate reason is for coming to it. Whatever may be true in various philosophies, we must settle in everyday life for little things. If we have someone's verbal commitment to an idea and at least a hope that he will follow it up with action, that should suffice. What people really think deep down is their business and should in most circumstances not enter into your calculations.

LOOKING OUT FOR YOUR INTERESTS

Nor, in a sense, should what you yourself think enter into your calculations. Let us say that you give your boss a lift to work every day. You are doing it because you live near her, and you like to be helpful. But you're also doing it because you are a brownnoser and are a little reluctant to face yourself for it. What of that? Nothing to be ashamed of. Why not curry favor? As long as doing so does not involve a compromise of your important principles, the fact that your giving her a lift has an ulterior motive is no disaster. *Why should you not look out for your interests?*

Besides, who is harmed by the action? The boss is happy to obtain a lift. You feel no great disability over doing it. Nor is the company necessarily being harmed by your getting the promotion a little more quickly this way. If you were a total incompetent, you would (in most cases) not have gotten the promotion, no matter what you did. But you are not incompetent, and if you did not perform this little favor, someone else might get the promotion before you, someone not necessarily better qualified than you.

Of course, if the boss is a criminal, a disreputable individual, or incompetent; if your actions on her behalf are sleazy, humiliating, illegal; if your consequent promotion involves double-crossing someone else, creating tensions, decreasing the effectiveness of the company—if one or all of these factors are present, your conscience might be well-advised to harass you. We talk now, however, of those numerous everyday actions that have no such gnawing overtones. In those cases, leave your motives alone. There will always be an ulterior motive lurking among them. If you do not bother with it, it will not bother you.

YOU DON'T HAVE TO BE A SAINT

The moral is that *you must learn to live with multiplicity of motives in yourself as well as in others and with doubts as to whether the real one can even be isolated.* You must cease brooding over your motives like a saint. A devout person who feels answerable to God for every action and thought is naturally much agonized over doing the right thing for the right reason. You don't have to be. If you are concerned with the salvation of your soul, fine. But if you are content with simply getting through each day and letting eternity look after itself, you don't have to be. Saints can control their actions but not their thoughts. This inability will cause them remorse, greater efforts to improve their thoughts, greater consciousness of mixed motives and failure, greater effort again, and so on. No matter how pious they become, they will be conscious of how far they still have to go. Even small feelings will be magnified, by their very isolation and rarity, out of all proportion.

To be human is to accept mixed motives

What is involved basically is accepting oneself— accepting human beings as peculiar animals with sometimes anti-social traits and minds that sometimes sink into the mud. You can think all sorts of things—murder and suicide and rape—*but not come near doing any of these things. Thought is free, quick, unpredictable, and uncontrollable.* Learn to live with that fact, and focus rather on your actions, on what you do that you shouldn't and what you don't do that you should. You must accept certain obvious verities:

1. All humanity is afflicted with mixed motives, low thoughts, uncontrollable wishes.

2. Even great individuals, conquerors like Napoleon or saints like St. Francis, lead an imperfect psychological life. As one sage said, Even the greatest persons on the highest thrones sit but on their asses.

3. You yourself, whatever you may believe about others,

are not exempt from the human condition. You too will harbor these thoughts. You must learn to accept yourself as a member of this human race, with kinship to both Napoleon and St. Francis, Hitler and Schweitzer. The difference is only that you won't act on—or react to—many of your thoughts as they did on theirs, which is only to say that you will not be a conqueror or saint, hero or villain. So what? You can live with that.

4. One of the effects of psychoanalysis is the tendency of some people to believe that the real you is not the face you present to other people, nor the personality expressed in your words and actions, but the hidden self discovered in dreams, secret thoughts, potential actions. Whether in fact your conscious mind or your unconscious is the real you is to be settled by philosophers and psychologists. Since the matter is debatable, the wise thing is to forget about it and go on the assumption that the real person is what you (and others) pretend and seem to be. Judge and be judged by words and actions rather than latencies, ulterior motives, and unconscious thoughts.

Ambivalence

A special version of mixed motives bothers many people—secretly. Just as we like to think that someone does, or should do, something for only one reason and at that a good reason, so do we believe that we hate some people and things and love others and that never the twain shall meet. Not so simple.

Psychologists have coined the term "ambivalence" to describe the simultaneity of love and hate. Such a coexistence has long been intuited by the great writers and thinkers. What is novel about the modern view is that according to it, we are ambivalent about *all* things.

Obviously, on some matters we do not show the contrary emotion. That remains our little secret. You love your parents, spouse, kids, country, religion, school, ideology, company, social club. "Love" means most of the time and outwardly, formally, officially, as far as you talk about the matter. According to the principle of ambivalence, some or much of the time and secretly, you also hate all these. And the stronger the love, the stronger the hate may be.

Similarly, you may dislike a neighbor down the street, a country, members of religions other than your own, schools competing with your own, or members of rival social clubs or of no social club. You may also hate promiscuous people, pornography consumers, homosexuals, intellectuals, political leaders. According to the doctrine of ambivalence, you sometimes and secretly love or at least envy them. You would like to be like or with or close to them.

How does ambivalence apply here? Very simply. *Sometimes you may find yourself hating those you love or loving those you hate*. You cower in shame and worry over what will happen, should anyone ever find out. Worse, *you feel yourself to be terribly guilty and a worthless person for harboring these thoughts. You cannot stand your repulsive self.*

Such a dilemma is nothing new to you, actually. As a child you were totally dependent on your parents, and all your love was centered on them. But there were times when they did things that drove you up a wall. Remember how embarrassed you were as a teenager when your parents began showing your baby pictures to all comers? How about the time that they refused to buy you a bicycle? You became angry, sometimes livid with rage. And running across your mind was the thought that you would be better off if your parents were dead. When your anger subsided, you felt guilt and shame about your thoughts.

LIVING WITH YOURSELF

You are not a freak or a peculiarly rotten person; on the contrary, you are perfectly normal. All those people out there, whatever their demeanor, are undergoing from time to time the same sort of mixed feelings and motives as you. They sometimes think of orgies and rape. They sometimes would like, in their heart of hearts, to torture and murder their enemies. They at various times hate some or all those closest to them. They periodically have selfish thoughts and ulterior motives and no motives.

Don't feel guilty. *Learn to accept and live with ambivalence*. It is only human, an inescapable fact of life, a universal. *It is a dirty little secret now exposed*. Even St. Francis probably had hours when he said to himself, "To hell with these stinking birds and fishes! They get on my nerves. Enough already!"

Feelings

PASSION

Embarrassment about motives and ambivalence ultimately turns out to be embarrassment about having any feelings at all. For motives are in good part feelings, and human beings are supposed to be decent, respectable, rational individuals, with few feelings or with feelings channeled into accepted modes of behavior. When they are not so channeled, you have mixed motives, ambivalence, pangs of conscience, and related ills.

A basic thrust of civilization has been to diminish the emotions, passions, desires. They are thought to be irrational, bestial, erratic, seductive, sinful, injurious to people, unscientific, disorderly, distracting. Such charges may be true, but the fact remains that the passions, however they may be reprehended, have their role to play, their place in the sun. Overlook that and the result is neurosis, inability to cope.

One large batch of ignored passions are the sexual ones. They are of immense importance, and not giving them recognition results in great unhappiness. Yet many people feel ashamed of sex, even though it is a natural drive, part of being human.

Take masturbation. Whatever one might say about other sexual practices thought to be deviant or abnormal, masturbation is a perfectly harmless act that—according to the educated conjectures of physicians and psychologists—probably no one has ever totally resisted for an entire lifetime.

The religious reprehend masturbation because of the sin of spilling seed. The psychologists, while denying the old religious proscriptions, proceed to replace them with new secular ones. The act is defective because it is narcissistic, they say, because a person hoards delight instead of sharing it, and because it does not involve a mutual fulfillment. More recent thinkers have discarded these shibboleths and hold that the emphasis on consistently shared rather than solitary experience is an unexamined assumption, an intellectual superstition.

Whatever the society and the people who mouth its dictates may say, masturbation is a pleasurable activity. Some activities should be shared; some not. There is a time to share and a time to be solitary. Not all people have the same inclination and capacities; and even among the sharers, some are not in a position or a mood to synchronize orgasms with anyone else.

The traditional view is—no marriage, no sex. Either get married or abstain. But common sense says that *although shared sex is sometimes superior to solitary sex, solitary sex is better than no sex.*

Even aside from all discussion about virtue and vice, harm and good, there is the simple moral imperative: Sexual activity is pleasurable; it therefore is good; and pleasure, when available—as it all too rarely is—should be seized. *Over masturbation hovers none of the anxieties that beset shared sex—venereal disease, pregnancy, emotional involvement and/or disruption.*

TEARS, NOT SO IDLE TEARS

Another pair of oppressed emotions are affection and grief. Many people in our society are ashamed to show their feelings. They do not like to hold hands or kiss in public; they sometimes feel inhibited even in private about using words like *love, infatuation, dependence, commitment.*

Affection

Some of this reluctance is justified. The overuse and misuse of these words, notably *love,* by our mercenary institutions have sometimes made them seem embarrassing and objectionable. A better toothpaste is alleged to make people "love" you. All sorts of letters are signed, "Love." For special occasions, we buy cards with prefabricated and often insincere expressions.

Still, the abuses should not sully the uses. If you love someone, say so. Stroke, hold hands, kiss—in public. You do not have to be lascivious or exhibitionistic about it, but there is a happy mean, an acceptable way of doing it.

Grief

The same applies to grief, perhaps even more so. Men are not allowed by our society to cry. Ever. The candidacy of Senator Edmund Muskie for the presidency some years back was ruined, many thought, because he cried in public over editorial abuse of his wife. Whether or not that incident played a major role in aborting his drive is beside the point; what is interesting is that so many people were sure that it did count heavily.

The taboo is ridiculous. Ancient heroes and conquerors—including angry Achilles, the heavyweight champion of the ancient world, and Alexander the Great—cried when the burden of life was too much for them. The sooner we get rid of this inhibition, the better. Of course, as with anger, there must be good reason and occasion for such a breach of everyday behavior and decorum. Crying over spilled milk, over things that can't be changed, over trivia, at inappropriate places and occasions, for too long, or too self-consciously is objectionable. It does not comport with the possibility of other options, of doing something about the loss. But crying in itself and at the proper juncture is not only not wrong; it is right, it is healthy, it is human, humane, *and manly*.

Anger

Another emotion with a bad press throughout history is anger. The earliest and perhaps still greatest work of literature in the Western world, Homer's *Iliad*, begins "Sing o

goddess of the anger of Achilles. . . ." The story proceeds
to relate how that wrath led to numberless deaths and how
a resolution of the problems it caused was not achieved
until Achilles learned to curb his temper. Everybody draws
the obvious inference from the story. Christianity considers anger one of the Seven Deadly Sins; philosophers insist
that it does not comport with wisdom and moderation;
modern people say that it has no place in a rational, scientific outlook.

Reality, as usual, is more complex than that. Even the
Christian theologians speak of "righteous indignation." So
it turns out that you *are* allowed to become angry, after all,
if the object of your wrath is the Devil or some human dis-
ciple of his.

The fact is that anger has its place in human life. To
suppress it is misguided. Frequent, immoderate, or
uncalled-for anger is bad, because it is self-defeating, not
because it is sinful or nonaltruistic. (Remember, the only
criterion is, Does something help you or not?) When you
blow up, you become irrational and say things that you
may later regret. The consequences of these outbursts are
that you have made yourself offensive, said stupid things,
and presented yourself as an individual who shouts first
and thinks later.

But when you give your friend your wallet to hold
and, upon your return, find that he took all the money out
without asking your permission; when you find that your
best friend went out behind your back with your boy
friend; when the boss promises you a raise but on the
looked-for day gives the raise rather to an incompetent rival; *in such cases, anger is called for and is healthy*. It is healthy
for you as an outlet, a safety valve, and healthy for the object of it in revealing how he or she did wrong and will not

perhaps do it again. Make the same point gently, as Christians and pacifists would have you do, and see if anyone listens or cares!

But before you do get carried away, *make sure that your anger is directed at the proper source*. Are you screaming at your girl friend because of what she did, or are you really angry at the low grade you got in biology but are unable to take your anger out on your teacher?

The Conniptor

Do not regard just any outburst as a healthy exercise of your anger muscle. One of the ways people have of dodging the truth is to get their priorities upside down and to become penny-wise and pound-foolish. They do not inquire into or try to control the really important matters, but you put a minor detail in their line of sight or scent and watch them connipt!

A Conniptor is a person who—throwing a fit over the fact that his or her spouse bought seats in the wrong part of the theater—is so wrought up over the seats and over the spouse's bad judgment that he or she sits through the season's smash play without hearing a line of it. A Conniptor is in spasms over a child's untied shoelaces but ignores the straight-A report card in the child's hand. A Conniptor accepts without a blink the inflated base sticker price of a brand new car but bashes his or her head against the wall over the price of white sidewall tires. A Conniptor decides to vote against a congressman for getting divorced but is indifferent to the congressman's stand on poverty, abortion, neutron bombs, the energy crisis. A Conniptor, finally, is one who—while spouse or kid has head stuck in the freezer—worries over the food thawing.

Conniptions come in all sizes and shapes, but what they have in common is a lot of sound and fury over trivia. You must ask yourself whether your rages are equal to the issue or whether you are not silent at all the wrong times. Anger is good only in its appropriate place. Otherwise, it is nothing less than foolishness.

CREATIVE STACK BLOWING

Anger is an important way of getting across the barriers we set up between each other. It is a form of force. When you arrive home and have your key, you open the door with the key. But when the key is—after all searches—lost, and you must get into the house fast, your only option is to use force. Do so. That is what anger is about. You cannot let people step all over you and take away your living space. You have to talk back, tell people why. Talk nicely, gently at first, perhaps twice or thrice. But if they do not listen, raise your voice. They will listen then. That is called anger. Perfectly useful and healthy activity.

Remember also that your anger is not hurting anyone. It is a mistake to think that the object of it is hurt. On the contrary, by letting others know how you feel, you give them a salutary lesson they probably would not obtain in any other way. And far from injuring you, it actually helps you, because by releasing your anger at once, you are getting it out of your system. Otherwise it will build up to resentment and sometimes even to destructive hatred.

As it is, you are angry with your offending friend. The friend recoils, sees that he or she did you wrong, and apologizes. You are placed in a forgiving mood, and before you know it, you are both friends again, but on a plane of understanding. Suppress your anger in order to retain the friendship, and the friendship will subsist on the basis of misunderstanding, deceit, and growing resentment on your part.

Of course, sometimes your outburst of anger will run into or arouse the anger of the person you are angry with, and then the sparks will fly. That may be unfortunate. Or it may be helpful, insofar as—like a summer thunderstorm—it clears the muggy air between you two. The point is not that anger is good but that it is not per se bad. Some anger *is* bad. *That anger sometimes leads to fights, physical or figurative, no more negates the usefulness of anger than does an occasional accident negate the automobile.*

Feelings are part of your individuality

Your feelings, then, like your ulterior motives and your ambivalences, are an essential part of you. In most clashes between the desire to express them and the obligation to adhere to the dictates of society or to the principle of good manners, your feelings must come first—*because they are feelings. And because they are yours.* To do anything else is to sacrifice your individuality on that obscure altar variously known as "society," "them," "duty," "others," "obligations," "responsibilities," "respectability."

11

Envy Is the Opium of Lazy People

One feeling is in special need of scrutiny: Envy. The others have merely to be rehabilitated, but this one needs to be clarified, refined, and put aside—or at least translated into effective action.

Envy is actually a classic case of unhappiness stemming not from selfishness but from a lack of selfishness or from a misdirected selfishness. Most people are too blind to be truly selfish. Instead of looking to themselves in forging a life-style, they bring irrelevant considerations into the equation. They make themselves unhappy by comparing themselves with:

a.   the way others are
b.   the way they themselves would like to be
c.   the way others would like to be.

By the time they get through with so much wrongheadedness, there is not much of the self left for them to lick their wounds.

THE URGE TO BE A XEROX COPY

Many people are guilty of the biblical sin of covetousness. In today's world, covetousness is wrong not because it is a sin or because some demanding deity prohibited it long ago, but because it is self-defeating and wasteful. What is the good of being irritated over the fact that while you struggled in class with a math problem, the girl next to you arrived at the solution effortlessly? What is the good of brooding on Charley's basketball prowess, Alice's way with men, Jane's thriving in real estate ventures, Clyde's talents as after-dinner speaker and politician?

You are not like them. Confront that reality once and for all, and get the resentment out of your system. Thinking on it week in and week out is not going to give you their talents, nor bring you happiness. A duck was not born to be a tiger, a tiger does not make it as an elephant, and an elephant would look silly trying to be a dolphin or a flamingo. It takes all kinds to make a world, and some things you were just not born or trained to do.

Once you get that rather obvious but often elusive fact into your head and heart, you face two choices. You can either improve your prowess in any of these fields to the point where you are a match for your friend. Or, failing that—and it *is* hard to become overnight a math whiz, a sexual swinger, a basketball star, or a wheeler–dealer— you can work harder at excelling at something that is more in line with your native talents. In other words, look at your assets and recognize that they can be made stronger. You may be no good at math, but you do have some talent in English or history. You may be no good at basketball,

but you are good at Ping-Pong or baseball. You will probably never be a great mathematician, a Joe Namath or a
Dustin Hoffman, a Casanova, F. D. Roosevelt, or J. Paul
Getty, but you may have it in you to be a good stamp collector, poker player, fisherman, or painter. These may not be
great things, but they are better than nothing. Excelling in
anything can be a source of pride or at least of ego resuscitation. The *Guinness Book of Records* has room for all sorts
of achievements, awesome or humble.

Comparing what you are not with what someone else is

*Instead of letting your potential talent drowse while you envy
the other person's feats, start working on what you can do well.*
Keep at it until, in maybe only a few months or a year, you
reach the point where Charley, Alice, Jane, and Clyde say
to you, "Wow, you can really do that well! Wish I was that
good at it."

Then you will have reached the point where you stop
envying them. They'll still be better than you at basketball,
socializing, real estate, and speech making, but you'll be
better than they are at someting else. You will feel good
then. You will see that it takes all kinds to make a world. If
you cannot be a tiger or an elephant, you can be a dolphin
or a swan.

One form of unhappiness does not come, then—as
moralists would have you think—from your being selfish,
but from your mistaken idea that all people were pro-
duced by a biological cookie cutter. It comes not from your
comparing yourself with somebody else but from your
comparing what *you are not* with what *someone else is*. That is
loading the dice against yourself. Unless you enjoy being
miserable—and there are people like that around too—
that is a silly way of operating.

Hardly any less ridiculous is the attempt to measure yourself *as you are* against *what you would be*. All of us naturally want to be the best in our field: a Louis Nizer or Edward Bennet Williams among lawyers, a Christiaan Barnard or Jonas Salk among doctors, a Sitting Bull among Indian chiefs. But just as tigers were not made to be elephants, so all tigers were not made of the same size, strength, and courage. You may have to settle for being a run-of-the-mill lawyer, machinist, teacher, electrician. Judge yourself and your success by standards that apply to you.

Are your standards realistic?

Are your standards realistic? Are you comparing your strength with that of a tiger? your skin thickness with that of an elephant? your height with that of a giraffe? You may never be a nationally known lawyer or the envy of your profession. But to your friends and close ones, you can be a success, because each of them has found something he or she needs and admires in you. One comes to you because of your understanding, another because of your cheerfulness or cooking skills or carpentry. Whether you are a teacher, accountant, or cabinet maker, to your immediate circle you are the expert, the one who knows the ropes. And this is where your real success and renown lie—in the ability to share an important part of yourself with others, not in dreaming of being someone you never can or will be.

Set goals that you can meet

Once you have done your best and know that you've done that, you will feel confident that you are among that

131

small percentage of people in this world who have given it their all; there is nothing to regret. Few people can be chief, but almost anyone can be a good brave, and yet that is no small feat: *A hundred-pound bantamweight who becomes a champion is doing better than a two-hundred-pound heavyweight who gets knocked out in the first round.*

You should, naturally, always try to do better. Do not rule out the possibility of reaching the heights some day. On the other hand, do not punish yourself with recriminations over not doing so. You should not push yourself beyond what is natural or rational. Don't get carried away with your wonderful qualities.

You may have overspecialized yourself. By devoting all your energies, let's say, to excelling in psychology, you may have neglected your English studies. But keep in mind that if you want to go to graduate school, you will need to develop your English skills, because as a budding psychologist you will be required to write reports, studies, and to analyze materials. Your writing capabilities may not be at the same level of achievement as your work in psychology, but writing skills are necessary tools if you are to become successful as a psychologist.

TAKING YOURSELF FOR A RIDE

The biggest folly is the one that combines the other two—regret over not being like *someone else* and regret over not being like *one's own dreams* for oneself: that is, regret over not being like *someone else's dream*. This surely is to go far afield from one's own range of resources and possibilities. If you allow yourself to fall into that trap, you will have a hard time getting out, because other people will, consciously or not, conspire to keep you there.

Although you may do a good job in one area, others may try to make you feel guilty for not doing what they expect of you. There are many institutions and people in our society who manipulate us in order to make us feel guilty for the way we are. We have all been, for instance, brought up with the belief that we have to honor our parents and respect their wishes. But what happens when their expectations for us are different from what we want for ourselves? It is true that our parents knew what was best for us when we were children, but is this true today?

You may want to go to a junior college and study for a technical career, but your parents have always dreamed of your entering one of the professions. When you do not accept your parents' expectations of you, they make you feel like a failure or an ungrateful child. The way out of this dilemma is not to automatically assume that you must be wrong and they are right. There is nothing wrong with parents having definite expectations for their children; however, it *is* wrong for your parents to expect you to lead your life according to their view of the world. If you think carefully, you will realize that the problem is not your selfishness but theirs.

Guilt for doing things in our own best interests

Or you may be a student in a dental technology program. Almost all the courses you are taking relate to your specialization. After school, you rush down to your part-time job. Between studying for your courses and your job, you have little time left over to socialize, go to concerts and museums. Your roommate accuses you of being a drudge and a limited person. He tells you that you have to expand yourself as a human being, that you can accomplish this by devoting less time to your studies, registering for more liberal arts courses, taking a greater interest in literature, art, and music. You know that it's silly, but every once in a while you ask yourself if you are really a drudge when all you are concerned with is not flunking out of school and having enough money to pay your tuition.

Such a situation is not a case of envying something somebody else has, or of your not living up to your own ideal, or of your not achieving as much as someone else does. *Because the chances are that your roommate himself is not living up to his own ideal, either.* Although he keeps telling you that you should work fewer hours at your job and that money is not important, he is receiving money from his parents to pay his tuition and living costs. He knows that according to his own ideals, he shouldn't do that. But he rationalizes that away by telling himself that in principle he believes that money is not important, that it only just so happens that his parents are well to do, and that it would be breaking his parents' hearts if he refused their generous offer. Anyway, he claims, were he forced to work to support himself, he would get an exciting and important job, still find time for çultural endeavors, and not be a money-pinching drudge like you.

The fact that he is willing to exempt himself from the sacrifices demanded by his principles makes it easier for him, by making you feel guiltier. Sure, you should expand yourself. It is important for you to take an interest in cultural activities. But it is also a fact that given your present circumstances, this is an unrealistic goal for you. Your predicament does not mean that you cannot do such things later. You can always take adult courses once you get your degree and in this way fill in the gaps in your education.

The visits to concerts, museums, and lectures may not

even be voluntary on your roommate's part. They may be part of class requirements. Yet he enunciates his definition of the cultured and self-actualizing man. Given human psychology, *the more he does not live up to his own principles, the more he will hold you up to them—not to your principles, but to his.* For your not living up to his principles, he will call you a drudge, a limited human being. And if you allow yourself to be brainwashed, you will be unhappy about your deficiencies vis-à-vis someone else's ideals.

Avoiding the guilt trip

The way out of this guilt trip is to think clearly. You have to realize that when choosing between the ideal good and the immediate good, you have a responsibility to protect yourself. If you don't, who will? It's all right for your liberal roommate to espouse his ideas, since he has the money and the multiplicity of options that money makes possible; but your circumstances are different.

RELIGIOUS GUILT

In the same way, healthy, vital young men and women growing up in a puritanical Jewish, Catholic or Protestant environment may find themselves stifled by the values of the community. To refrain from premarital sexual experience or to feel severe guilt over infractions of this sort is to make oneself unhappy over not living up to *other people's* ideals.

Asceticism is fine for those with anemic passions, for those who only enjoy studying ancient books or contemplating religious painting. No one would want to deny such people their asceticism. Mankind should excel in every way, and it is as exhilarating to see a human being able to get through 365 days of the year without yielding once to sexual temptation as it is to see someone run a three-minute mile or walk on the moon.

Not all people, however, can be satisfied with the ascetic life. The trouble with the religious systems is that they expect self-denial from everyone, uniformly. They expect young people with normal and healthy sexual drives to stifle those drives. They expect modern youth to live up to the standards set down by Middle Eastern ascetics long ago. A universal, absolute moral code forces people onto the Procrustean bed, where the legs of some are stretched and those of others chopped off. To abide by such a code against one's deepest desires and for reasons long obsolete—antiquated notions of virginity, purity, honor—is to be ruled by other people's ideals.

Media fantasies

If traditional religion makes you miserable for shortcomings in one direction, modern advertising (and life as portrayed in movies and television) makes you miserable for shortcomings in exactly the opposite direction. Religion damns you for yielding to lustful thought, and advertising and motion pictures damn you—the modern version of damnation is to make you feel inferior and inadequate—for *not* yielding to lustful thoughts.

The major religions, after all differences have been accounted for, object to the Seven Deadly Sins—pride, gluttony, lechery, sloth, envy, wrath, despair. Modern advertising celebrates and tries to arouse our response to precisely these seven sins. It makes you feel that you're missing out on the action if you don't fly with Georgette to the Bahamas, if you don't wear clothes that have the name of a famous French designer all over them, if you don't own a famous Japanese stereo or German sports car, if you don't swoon over Sammy Davis in Las Vegas. It would even have you believe that if you don't use a particular beer, mouthwash, or toothbrush, you are forfeiting a scandalously successful sex life.

To grow up in some sort of religious environment in modern times, as most people still do, is therefore to be vulnerable on two fronts. You are made to feel bad for not living up to two different sets of values. Since the two sets happen also to be flatly contradictory, you are trapped. Your predicament will accordingly remain hopeless until you remember to be selfish—that is, to live for yourself and not for *other people's ideals*.

ENVYING CELLULOID IDEALS

Sometimes, of course, you can't differentiate between your own ideals and those of others. The society has done such a thorough job of brainwashing that they become one. That is at the heart of the marital problem in America. It is no coincidence that the country with the highest divorce rate also contains Hollywood and long propagated the mythology of the "lived-happily-ever-after" marriage found in so many movies.

Generations of men and women have been sent out into life with imaginations hobbled (by movies) with illusions about love and marriage. In the basic story line, a handsome young man meets, often by chance, a ravishingly beautiful young woman. After some adventures and adversities, they come together and walk hand-in-hand into the sunset. Ahead lies marriage and eternal bliss.

Whatever problems life presented were settled in bringing the couple together, and none was left over. The music swells to a climax, the credits flash on the screen, the curtains close, the theater lights go on, and the audience walks out into the briefly painful daylight feeling that they have beheld the basic pattern of love. They eagerly await the moment when that pattern will overtake them, when lightning will strike for each of them.

The plot was blissfully uncomplicated by such matters as premarital sex, or the feeling peculiar to the morning after the wedding day or honeymoon. No hint is given as to who will take out the garbage, as to the boredom on the job, the tensions of living together with *anyone* else, the divergent sexual rhythms, the coping with the daily household drudgery, the dying out or at least alteration of love. Nothing in the movie suggests that love ultimately has little to do with physical beauty, which is transitory in any case. Nothing hints at the strengths and weaknesses of love, the problems and obstacles, or at such ingredients of marriage as mutual understanding, harmony through adjustment, a desire to do things for the spouse, an ability to undergo self-sacrifice.

Given the power of the enlarged movie-screen image over us and its powerful impact on our emotions, such a reiterated message has left numerous young people unprepared for marriage and middle-aged people confused about their own motley relationships. How many set out looking for a lover who resembles Elizabeth Taylor, Raquel Welch, Clark Gable, or Robert Redford? How many proceed to bring the same impossible expectations to bear on every step of the courting process? Hence some find it impossible ever to marry, and many who do get past this hurdle find it necessary to divorce.

The message is clear. Ask yourself, Are the private lives of the stars as good as the roles they play? Then you can stop looking for Raquel Welch and stop feeling inferior to Robert Redford. Though you may not look like Redford, you may have certain strengths of character or intellect that he lacks; and if you stop looking for a nonexistent Raquel, you may find instead a girl who has just the sensitivity to discern what most people don't— those strengths of yours that Redford lacks.

To think of love in Redford–Raquel terms is about as sensible as believing the stories of sexual conquests told at the corner bar or in the locker room. The Hollywood version is, in fact, the fantasy of people of all ages who never grew up. To believe in it is to retard oneself. To believe in it is once again to ruin one's life by trying to live up to other people's—in this case, immature people's—ideals.

12

Sweet and Sour Grapes

Defusing things

If envying other people is not turned into a springboard for action, it can become a destructive force in your system. But another remedy is available: treating it with the special care reserved for setbacks and frustrations. These come in many forms, even to the giants of history, perhaps especially to them, since they take many large risks. This chapter discusses areas of your lives in which setbacks are likely to occur, how to view these setbacks, and what steps you can take to overcome them.

Interpersonal relations

One area where people particularly make a mess of things is in interpersonal relations. Although we make many mistakes in our estimation of the world and our handling of life situations, our options in relating ourselves to abstractions like the school, the job, the political situation, the universe, are limited. We can do only so much by way of altering the state of things and improving our conditions. Our relations with our parents, friends, and relatives, on the other hand, are both more important to us and, fortunately, more amenable to change. However narrow our choices may be in other fields, when it comes to personal relations we are free agents—if we only knew it. This may seem like limited freedom, but as the old joke has it, "In my family, I worry about important matters like foreign policy, the economy, the state of the arts, while my wife worries about unimportant matters, like which car we will buy, when to renovate the house, how much to spend on clothing this year, whether to send the kids to private or public school." The point is, of course, that these "unimportant" things matter greatly to the individual.

DEALING WITH PARENTAL DEMANDS

Take the case of the young man or woman who feels put upon because his or her parent keeps on wanting to receive a phone call every day. Living by yourself, you naturally feel constrained by a demand of that sort. It makes you feel as though you were still tied by the apron strings to the parent, were still an incompetent kid who has to be reminded to wash behind the ears and to report back to one's mother or father every day what you are doing. You are even more ashamed about having to do so when you suspect that your friends are not hemmed in by *their* parents, who are surely less demanding.

Do not worry about what others are doing

How cope with this problem? To begin with, you should not worry about your friends, not only on this subject but on any. You do entirely too much of that. Forget about conforming to the mores of the average person, the crowd. You should worry rather about relating things to yourself, to your own notions of right and wrong.

If you look into it closely, you might find that your friends are actually undergoing the same problems and are no nearer a solution than you. Only they are doing a good job of keeping things tightly under their hats. It is possible that we have here a situation of a lot of people coping with the same problem but all thinking that they are unique and wondering what the others would say if they knew, when in fact what the others would say is, "Welcome aboard!" or "You, too!" or "Isn't it funny the way we're all in the same boat."

Your choices

YOU ARE NOT GOING TO CHANGE YOUR PARENTS

There are immutable elements in the situation. You are not going to change your parents at this late stage in their lives. You can, to be sure, bring the matter to a head by making a principled stand and informing them that you are a grown-up now and that they are going to have to do with fewer phone calls. This may free you of the burden of having to make those daily calls, but it will also lead to an explosion and a breakdown of relations. That may be fine—no more phone calls for a while—but it will leave your parents feeling terrible and you feeling guilty over their feeling terrible. Then, after an interlude, there will be all the hassle of reconciliation, the feelers through intermediaries, the apologies and requests for forgiveness, the tearful scenes—who needs all that? And then, after another, shorter interlude, you will be right back where you were, with the parent demanding more frequent—if not daily—phone calls from you, and you resenting it and being ashamed. So that is not a very effective way of doing things.

Grit your teeth?

As to the problem itself, you have various choices. You can stop calling and make the parent call you. You can continue to call every day with teeth gritted.

A better approach would be for you to defuse the emotional charge by squaring things with yourself. You need not, in other words, feel so bad over still having this close relationship with the parent. It is not unhealthy, and it is something that, in any case, cannot be helped. So live with it and make the most—or the least—of it. *Instead of defining "mature" as not phoning one's parents too often, you should redefine it as not making much ado over having to phone one's parents daily, if that is what they want.* You are not going to sit down and cry over not having wings? Then why fret over having to call your parents every day? Not to call them might be like having wings; but just as you do not have physical wings, so must you be kept landborne by having to defer to and take account of your parents.

The way to handle this problem is to defuse the anger. Treat it as merely another perfunctory task to be gone through every day, along with many others. No one complains about having to attend to laundry every few days, about having to shop for groceries, about having to spend an hour in the subway each workday. A major portion of your day is spent in such perfunctory tasks, and although you can reduce the time spent on them somewhat, you cannot eliminate the need. So calling your parents when you have nothing to tell them is merely another of each day's perfunctory tasks. No use making a major production out of it.

Draw up a schedule

Compromise with your parents; draw up a schedule that makes allowance for such calls. Call every other day instead of every day. Distance yourself a little bit, far enough to take some of the psychic pressure off you and let you feel like an independent, dignified adult, but not too far lest they feel that you are abandoning them and embroil you in one of those noisy, futile squabbles. Whether the frequency of calls be reduced to every other or third or fourth day, some face-saving compromise, some easy way out, can be found. The important thing is to tell yourself that some things have to be gone through and that you should not let them get to you.

Do it and get it over with, rather than—by brooding over it—making it smear the rest of the day as a snail leaves a track in its wake. By persuading yourself that it does not matter, that parents have to be humored, that no one else need know—you are removing the emotional component of the relation and simplifying it. Quite a few things in life affect us that should not.

Sour grapes

There are many other things that we want and that are unattainable. Many of us dispose of such problems by the principle of Sour Grapes. It works very simply. You want something. You cannot have it. So you tell yourself that what you wanted is no good anyway, shrug your shoulders, and walk away. You have put the matter behind you.

To religious leaders, philosophers, and psychologists, such a procedure is bad, even evil. Such "rationalization"—giving a reason that sounds good but is not the true motive—involves lying, cheering oneself up with illusion. The grapes may in fact be very sweet, but you find it easier to get by with the fantasy that they are sour.

In the abstract we would agree that, other things being equal, one should cleave to the accurate description of reality. In practice, however, most people are not purists, philosophers, and idealists. They are vulnerable creatures, and telling little white lies to themselves not only makes things more pleasant and easy for them but may be an important ingredient in their functioning. We are, in any case, not saying that you *should* do this, only that you need not feel guilty over doing it. It is a crutch of which most people avail themselves, no matter what idealists say. You can have too much of a good thing, even of the truth. *If the truth can never be arrived at and is in good part a condition of your assumptions and of your circumstances, it is more important to get into the right circumstances than to waste time looking for an elusive truth.* The way you cope with setbacks is an important indication of that.

On being rejected

Let us say that you wanted to marry a particular person and you are turned down. You are crushed. You may choose now to dwell on your love's superlative qualities and become thereby incapacitated for further socializing. Any other individual you meet is deficient, compared to

your great love.' Having become fixated on it, you are
closed to further love; you are even paralyzed.

The alternate response, which many people make, is
one of what is called "bouncing back." They begin to dwell
on their love's deficiencies, persuading themselves that
that individual would not have been such a great mate
anyway. Rationalization? Possibly. But look at the result.
This rationalization enables them to put their former love
behind them and to go out vigorously seeking new love
and perhaps a lover who *will* have them.

MOVING TO NEW EXPERIENCES IS SUPERIOR
TO MOPING ABOUT PAST FAILURES

One point to remember is that rationalizing to oneself
when something else can be done is indeed harmful and self-
defeating, but many cases of sour grapes involve situations
where *nothing can be done* and where rationalizing to oneself opens new doors and possibilities. Idealists can prate
all they want, but moving on to new challenges and possible achievements is far superior to moping about past failure. If a lie about the grapes being sour is the necessary
catalyst for action, so be it. That is a small price to pay. Besides, it often is not such a big lie anyway. As Oscar Wilde
pithily put it, the only thing worse than not getting what
you want is getting it.

Who needs a throne of gold anyway?

If Sour Grapes enable you to continue on life's way
even in the face of defeat, so also is the opposite procedure
necessary, that of Sweet Grapes. Telling yourself that
things beyond your grasp are probably no good—even

though you may not know that for certain—is balanced by telling yourself that things *within* your grasp are the best you can have or can do.

Sweet grapes are not, therefore, so much the opposite of Sour Grapes as an extension of them. For you will have an easier time dismissing the grapes beyond your reach as sour *if you have concurrently grapes within your reach to turn to and can tell yourself that those grapes are good*. Sweet Grapes simply means seeing the importance of what you have or what is in your reach.

As Shakespeare put it, "A poor thing but mine own." This statement can be read as a pessimistic acknowledgment that what you have is pitiful but because it is yours, it is something anyway. Or as a *proud acknowledgment that, because it is yours, its pitifulness is unimportant*. Sweet Grapes dictates that since both readings are equally strong, you adopt the latter. *The cup is half full rather than half empty*. The fact that the object—be it a toy or a presidency, a spouse or a bike—is yours makes it more important than that it is poor; the fact that it is yours means that, for you, *it stops being poor*. "A bird in the hand is worth two in the bush." "A half a loaf is better than no loaf."

We err in esteeming things by some objective, external, absolute criteria of worth. Nothing can be so assessed; all things are relative. Diamonds are expensive because they are relatively rare, whereas milk is cheap. In a society where diamonds might be plentiful and pasteurized milk rare, the one would come cheap and the other expensive.

The worth of an object is its value to you

Therefore stop worrying about the value of something in itself, and start worrying about its *value to you*—meaning whether it can become a part of your life. If it is beyond your reach, do not waste your energies in fantasies about it, and concentrate rather on things within your reach. Assess things by whether you can have them, what good they are to you, how relevant they are to your means, capacities, plans, and life-style. *An easy chair that you can afford is much more important, useful, pleasing than a throne made entirely of gold*. That *is sweet grapes*.

As Oscar Wilde defined the cynic, "He is a man who knows the price of everything and the value of nothing." To call something "poor" means giving its price—that is, what the world thinks of it and nothing of what the thing means to you. What it means *to you* is its real value, not what others are willing to pay for it. What good is an all-gold throne if you cannot afford to buy it, to safeguard it, and you have no room in your apartment to put it? It has a high price and is highly prized, but being useless to you, it is without real value and should not obtain from you so much as a thought.

You must look at value rather than price. You must consider how things affect you rather than how they affect others. You must entertain not the absolute worth of the thing, if that is even possible, but the relevance it has to you.

The impossible dream is—impossible

In order to consider how things affect you rather than how they affect others, you must first assess yourself. What are your aims? What is your goal? The answer many people give is, "Excellence." *Why Not the Best?* is the title of President Carter's book. "Winning is the only thing," said a famous football coach. The thrust of American culture and modern society is to go ever upward and onward to bigger and better heights. Excelling is a positive goal. But as with most dictates, such advice should be taken in moderation. Know your limits.

HITTING SINGLES OR STRIKING OUT

Your first reaction is likely to be, "Why sell myself short? Why not go for excellence?" That reaction is caused by the rhetoric and brainwashing in our society. If you really had the knack to be a home-run hitter, you would have already worked on your swing. *The choice is not*, as you deem it, *between hitting home runs and hitting singles*. If it were, you would be right to go for the big ones. *The choice rather is*, if you would only own up to it, *between hitting singles and striking out*! Home runs are simply not an option for you. Now that is a different picture. Which is the more valuable player, someone who swings for home runs and connects maybe once in every ten games, with luck, or the individual who goes for singles and gets a pair in every game?

A major first step, consequently, is to find out where your talents are and then adjust your sights accordingly. Are you a slugger, a potential home-run hitter who can really send that ball flying? If the signs are clear that you are, by all means swing for the fences. If the signs are that you are not, or even if the signs are ambiguous, wisdom would dictate that you concentrate rather on doubles and singles and bases on balls. Even Babe Ruth was first a great pitcher and then a home-run hitter, not both at the same time.

STRIVING FOR PERFECTION

One writer has told a story of a man who had a lovely wife but who was upset by a birthmark on her cheek that took a little away from her facial perfection. He could not rest content until he subjected her to a treatment that removed the imperfection. The treatment worked all right;

it removed not only the birthmark, but also her life. Unable to live with imperfection, he achieved perfection only in death. No sweet grapes there. A rich thing, he was in effect saying, but not—as long as she had the birthmark—his own.

Letting go

The great secret is therefore to learn the art of "Letting Go." You must become like the chess master who knows when to jettison his grand strategy or like the circus trapeze artist who knows when to release her hands.

TO BE OR NOT TO BE—ROCKEFELLER

The importance of "mine own" (in Shakespeare's phrase) cannot be overlooked, either. People often say or think, "Gosh, I would like to be a Rockefeller or a Joe Namath." They are making a serious error. Being Rockefeller means no longer being yourself, with your particular habits, tastes, and values, and becoming instead someone utterly different. It means in effect committing suicide. Surely here is the ultimate in counterproductiveness and self-destructiveness that an untutored envy can lead you to.

What people really mean when they say that they would like to be Rockefeller is that they would like to *have Rockefeller's wealth, not actually be Rockefeller.* Or as a nightclub comic used to say, "I don't want to be a millionaire—I just want to live like one!"

The fact that something—a life no less than a hat—is your own gives it a certain dignity in your own eyes, even if in no one else's. No matter what adversities have happened to you—wasted or missed opportunities—you must believe that what happened is ultimately meaningful, just because it happened to you and to no one else. No matter how bad the adversity, you chalk it up to experience and thereby salvage something from it. "A poor thing but mine own." You have learned from the defeat, and you won't make that mistake again, even if you will make other mistakes.

That experience has affected you in a way peculiar to you and contributes further to your uniqueness. That sense of having learned something, of growing in wisdom, gives you a feeling of continuity, growth, and pattern in your life. It gives you a vested interest in your identity. "However average is my life," you say to yourself, "it's still *my* life and therefore the most precious thing in the world. These grapes are to me, because they are mine, sweet— even if admittedly with a tart edge to them."

Just as believing, rightly or wrongly, the grapes beyond one's reach to be sour enables one to accept defeat and move on to other, graspable endeavors, so believing the grapes in your possession to be, rightly or wrongly, sweet enables one to remain on good terms with oneself. *Sour grapes ease the way to new challenges; sweet grapes enable you to continue with familiar tasks.*

13

Why Let Words
Do the Talking
for You?

Words, acts, and facts

In defining the problem people face and formulating possible solutions, we confront the question of the relation of language to reality, of words to actions. Philosophers and poets worry such matters to death sometimes, whereas nonphilosophers and nonpoets are not even aware of the distinction. As in the case of assumptions, we would not bother with it, did it not play an important role in the day-to-day life of people, in the possibility of contentment, in the problem of coping.

Words are to things as money is to work, or checks to money. They are a shortcut, a pinch hitter, an acceptable substitute. They simplify life by making it possible to describe or change someone's physical environment without acting out that description or change. It certainly is a lot easier to say, "I wish I had a hundred pounds of gold," than to go through all the difficulties of obtaining a hundred pounds of gold, miming the message, and then returning the hundred pounds to the person from whom you borrowed it in order to make the point that you did not have it.

So far, so good. As long as words are in some way the photographic and tape-recorded image of reality, they work. As a result, we work, civilization works. But what happens when the packaging does not fit the content, when words are not the duplicate of things? What happens when the label says *Red Salmon* and the can turns out to contain only pale cat food?

Such things happen sometimes, because somebody made a mistake. The company expresses its sincere regret about the mislabeling and gladly gives the consumer double his money back. At other times, a shady company deliberately mislabels its products and tries to pass off cat food on the unwary as high-quality salmon; rather as people deliberately say things that are not so in order to part you from your money, your chastity, or your reputation. In that way a salesperson says, "This can opener is good for your lifetime," when she knows it will fall apart before the leaves of autumn descend; a seducer says, "I love you," when he knows he will be miles away before he sleeps; a slanderer says, "Jim shoots up on dope," because he hates Jim. A simple name for this is "lying."

BLACK LIES, WHITE LIES, AND LIES TO ONESELF

Villains like Hitler lie every time they turn around. Even on a less notorious level, every group of people contains at least one person whom the others know not to trust because he or she is a congenital, chronic, pathological liar. This individual may not have the ambition of a Hitler on behalf of which to do the lying; he or she lies for its own sake.

People like that are fortunately a small minority. What about the rest of us? We like to think of ourselves as honest and decent. Are we? We cannot remember when we last lied, but a little self-observation can show that few of us manage to get through the day without lying a few times. Some people are shocked to make this discovery. They need not be. Only in heaven can one lead a saintly life. Some lies are not only unavoidable but even advisable. No need to tell an eager boy friend proud of his new tie that it, frankly, stinks.

Some lies are objectionable albeit even more unavoidable—the lies to oneself. These are among the hardest to see for what they are. These are the lies discussed in the early chapters, those illusions that you have of knowing yourself, of regarding yourself as both inferior and superior, as alone and as not alone, as open-minded and eager for the truth—all the things that are called being out of touch with oneself, not in contact with one's feelings. You feel one way and believe another, think this but do that. Yet you are not at all aware of any discrepancy. You even are, in one more display of lack of self-awareness, angry with those bringing the problem to your attention.

The lying that involves deceiving others for your own advantage is a relatively simple kind. In most cases, people soon enough come to see through the chronic liar and hypocrite.

Talking one way and acting another

The problem is with those unaware that they talk one way and act another. A lot of people do some of that; some do a lot of that. Here are five examples of this dislocation.

1. Words instead of Deeds. In a crisis, you offer words in lieu of deeds. You always commit yourself to doing good. You have not the heart to say no to any request, even though you have not the slightest intention of doing anything to back your words. You are not insincere, but you feel or hope that pious words may even make actions unnecessary. If a friend has difficulty paying the rent, you ask, "Do you need any money?" These words seem as good as actually writing out a check. You feel cowardly or ashamed before people; you are so worried about your present reputation that you will not worry about your long-range reputation. You are insecure, especially in conversation. So you say "yes" to whatever people ask of you, but you make no plans to implement anything nor ever do anything. People learn eventually to disregard your word, but there are always new people coming along, always new hopes in people.

2. Words before deeds. You intend to do what you say, but you are sluggish, and time erodes your will. You have promised a friend help with his or her studies. By the time you have to redeem your promise, you forget having made it, or you think you qualified it with "if," "when," "maybe." Or you are sure that conditions have changed. You are tired, and anyway he or she does not need your help anymore. Your intentions were real, sincere; but they have a way of wandering off.

If you fall into one of these two categories, you had better get a grip on your language. *In the long run, empty words are much more offensive than dirty words.* In some few junctures and with a few sapheads, words will do as a substitute for deeds, but not in most cases. To add to the already widespread and confusing wrenching of language and deeds is to make things difficult for yourself and your acquaintances and in turn to make yourself obnoxious to them.

Healthy candor is best

If you cannot help someone, say so. You will find that it is not as painful as it may at first seem. And even if it is, in the long run, people have respect for healthy candor and self-interest and contempt for syrupy evasiveness, insincerely proclaimed altruism, and no-show commitments. If you are sincere but allow time to erode your will, next time you commit yourself, make doubly sure you follow through, lest a bad routine sets in. And then do so again. And again, *until it becomes a habit, not a chore*.

3. Words preventing action. One big hurdle to altering your life is the bad habit of complaining about everybody and everything. Though the opposite of envy, bitching is in a curious way mixed up with it; you are in some secret fashion envious of the alleged racketeering and success and malingering of those you complain about.

Everyone knows the litany. Politicians are whores. Doctors are highway robbers. Lawyers are shysters. The educational system is manned by overpaid incompetents. The police are crooked. Children are horrendous nowadays. Jews are pushy, Blacks are lascivious, the Irish are drunken brawlers, the Italians are mafiosi, the WASPS are unemotional and manipulative. Everybody is rotten to the core.

Psychic crutches

The first thing to note about this familiar syndrome is that it is only a generalization. The second thing is that it is a self-serving piece of cant, which gets you off the hook and glorifies you. The third and most important observation is that it is basically a gigantic cop-out and rationalization. It is a special form of both wish and fear fulfillment. Immersed in your pessimism, cynicism, and nihilism, you feel justified in not doing anything about either the world or your life.

Before you can change your life, you must change your thinking and discard those pseudoideas. *Such complaints tell us little about the world around you but a lot about the world inside you.* Constituting psychic crutches rather than social observation, they have psychological, not sociological, importance. They are a part—more effect than cause—of your problem, and throwing them away as useless crutches will be part of the solution.

4. Words and the low art of kvetching. Notice the self-contradictions you perpetrate when you presume to see everything but in fact look at reality only from your own limited perspective. How often have you heard yourself, or someone else, complain about the cost of living? "Five dollars for a movie ticket! It used to be two!" ". . . Fifty cents for an ice cream cone! It used to be twenty five cents!"

This is a half-truth. Some goods and services have indeed become unduly expensive, and we all know what they are: medical care, college tuition, heating oil. Others have, however, remained the same in price or actually gone down over the long haul: plane travel, long-distance phone calls, chickens, flour, TV sets, calculators.

The good old days

The main point not to miss is that if the overall cost of living has gone up, so has income, and often more quickly than the cost of living. A movie ticket may cost $5 instead of $2 and a dinner out $15 a head instead of $8, but you ignore the fact that when people were paying $8 and $2 for dinner and a movie, they were making lower salaries. *Many people conveniently forget how exorbitant the $2 and $8 seemed at the time.* If the good old days were not all that good, the bad days now cannot be all that bad, or at least they are not much worse.

So also do many people rail continually against the Society, the System, or the Establishment. *We are not by any means saying that you should not try to change the world. On the contrary, we are helping you try to do so.* One way of not changing the world is to rail and kvetch. *A practical alternative is to first try to understand why things are the way they are; there are usually good reasons.* Only then can you investigate whether or not there is room for maneuvering, whether a little movement in one direction or the other might not improve things without incurring new or greater risks. Life, like politics, is the art of the possible. *Instead of dwelling on why something won't work, try to find a way of making it work.* Anything is better than passive kvetching.

A SENSE OF APPROPRIATENESS

You get what you pay for

You need a sense of appropriateness. You ignore or forget that if you want the best in food or service, you have to go to an expensive place; and if you want to save money, you must be prepared for less than the best. There are, as the saying has it, no free lunches. The decision as to whether you should save money or have fancy service depends on your values and taste, no less than on your financial condition. An exhibitionist would say go to the expensive place; a moralist would say go to the cheap place. But *you* must decide, and whatever your choice, a price will have to be paid as surely as benefits are to be had. Hence complaining when you have the options and consequences clearly spelled out is futile and silly.

5. Words as wish fulfillment and fear fulfillment. Although the dislocation of words and deeds can be deleterious, it can also bring about a regeneration in the personality—that is, *when words are the beginning of, rather than the substitute for, action.* People have a way of dismissing something by saying, "It's only words!" Some "only"! Words have turned the world upside down and influenced people's lives in more ways than can be imagined. Nor must one underestimate the power and effect of words in everyday life.

The wish is father to the thought

It is a common observation that "the wish is father to the thought" and that, in turn, thinking or wishing something to be so may sometimes bring it about, that one may talk oneself or events into being. Though some of this is plain primitive superstition, there is enough truth to it to affect personal relations, positively and negatively. If you call yourself the world's greatest and act as though you mean it, as Muhammed Ali did in the past two decades, it is conceivable that you may achieve things that you might not have otherwise.

Lest it appear as simply boasting, you have to have something your words can work with. You have to be potentially championship material, and then your word campaign, your self-puffery, your boasting and pride may be just the stuff to push you over the top.

No boasting but active change

Conversely, a ninety-pound weakling is not going to go far if the best he can do is mope about being what he is. People will take him at his own word. *If you do not like what you are, do not dwell on that, especially with others, but on what you could be and on how you propose to reach it.* Push your thoughts, words, *and actions* hard enough, and you just might get there.

Going further

"Right you are—if you think you are," said a playwright, and that remark applies as well to behavior: "You *can* win if you are sure you will." Jesus implied that those of faith could walk on water. No one appears to have taken him up on it, but is that a judgment on the incorrectness of his words or on the lack of people with sufficient faith? You really have to believe in your own capacity, and one way of doing that is to boast, to give yourself a high standard to reach, to reread your résumé with its list of achievements so far. If you have come as far as you have, who says you cannot go further?

Words cannot be the end. They must be the beginning, to be followed by belief and actions. They have a way of becoming beliefs or, if springing from semibeliefs, of turning into full beliefs. Beliefs will in turn have the same curious relationship with actions.

By the same token, letting fears govern your thoughts may help bring about what is feared. Psychologists speak of wish fulfillment: You want to win someone's love or pass an exam, and so you dream of having done so and then wake up regretfully to discover that your fantasy had run ahead of reality. One can as easily speak of fear fulfillment. For just as often do you dream of disaster—of not getting the beloved or of flunking the test. Though the causes of the inaction lie elsewhere in the psyche, you exploit these fears as rationalizations for inaction.

By dwelling too long and much on adversity and defeat, you contribute to bringing it about. You become resigned to it; you lose your will to struggle; you prefer the predictable to the unknown. That is why in combat of any sort, one of the first responsibilities of the leader is to diminish or suppress news of setbacks and magnify news of victory. If it looks like you are on the way to victory or defeat, the words you choose—and not necessarily the facts—may accelerate the trend. To let fear rule you is to make the fear official and entrenched. To predict disaster may be a way of incurring it. So why, indeed, let the wrong words do the talking for you?

14

Drowning
in
Things

Harvesting machines

As modern Americans, we are heirs to two separate traditions that bring the same pressure to bear on us. One is
the American need to innovate, build, accumulate, prosper. The other is the modern Western industrial culture
of creature comforts, of accumulating gadgets and labor-
saving devices. These two have blended so nicely that
Western technology has enabled American activism to
make prodigious achievements. Everywhere we are associated with *the "good life," meaning not moral or religious
goodness but the life of goods*.

Everyone raised in America has been taught to accumulate goods. And what a flood of goods! Among large
"necessities" are cars, TV sets, refrigerators, air condition-
ers, washers, dryers, dishwashers, humidifiers, dehumid-
ifiers, hot-water heaters, power lawn mowers, stereos,

quadraphonic sets, mopeds, CB radio, tape recorders. Then there are thousands of smaller items, and there is duplication.

NECESSARY OR SUPERFLUOUS?

Many of these things are or have become important. A car may have been a luxury once, but our social arrangements—the growth of suburbs, the distancing of place of work from place of residence, the decline of mass transit systems—have made a car a necessity. So has it been with many of the other items on the list. If not as yet necessary, they are at least labor saving and helpful. A washer and a dryer in the basement to which one has recourse at any time of day or night are surely an improvement on having to wash one's clothes manually or having the laundryman come by once a week to pick up the family's dirty clothes.

So far, so good. The modern American system seems to work nicely. Still, some hitches developed in the process: (1) the means often become the end; (2) the labor saving device creates labor; (3) the drive to accumulate things becomes a goal in itself and a bad habit. The conjunction of these wrinkles causes no little unhappiness.

The means often become the end

THE CAR AS A JEWEL

The automobile is a device meant to move you quickly from here to there so that you can pursue those activities that make life meaningful. It saves you time otherwise lost by using mass transit or by walking.

But what happens every other year when you buy not a car but a jewel? You spend hours in showrooms worrying over color combinations, lavish interior, the sound of car stereo or car doors, the ritzy look of hubcaps and white sidewall tires. What happens when you then spend a good part of each third or fourth weekend—especially in the grimy city—washing and polishing the car? And how about repairs? Instead of saving you time, the car is beginning to take up more of it than would be the case if you simply took mass transit.

Machines do save time, but not as much as you may think. Remember that if you count only the work rendered unnecessary by the machines, you are cheating; you must include the work *created* by the machines. The pluses and minuses then may not be so clear. To calculate only the hours saved by using the car rather than mass transit is to overlook also the hours of work put into driving the car, hours the mass transit user can devote to reading, studying, writing. So purchase a car if you must, *but be sure that it remains your servant and does not become a master.*

The labor-saving device creates labor

Suppose you make $15,000 a year. Something like two-thirds goes for taxes and living expenses, and the remaining third can be used for first-class travel; for cooling it on the beaches of Acapulco, Fire Island, the Riviera, or Tahiti, or for gourmet meals. That is, if you are leading a relatively machineless life. If you insist on having labor-saving devices, however, you'll be paying for them out of that last third of your income. That means that instead of high-style leisure you have to stay home and mind, or mend, your air conditioners, washers, stereos, and cars. That may be a choice you're willing to make—having year-round general convenience and comfort rather than a month of high living far away. Nothing silly about such a choice.

But suppose your income is $15,000 and you have four kids. Any purchases of cars, extra air conditioners, and TVs—and with four kids, you'll need extra TVs and air conditioners—can no longer come out of money otherwise usable in Acapulco. There is no money left over. Just getting by, with tuna casseroles instead of steaks, consumes your $15,000.

So the machines can be obtained in only one of two ways: taking out loans or working overtime. "Working overtime?" Does that mesh with "labor-saving devices?" Moonlighting nights and weekends on a second job so that you can affort to buy extra cars and machines which supposedly will make life easier and extra TV sets which you yourself will rarely have the time to use—it's beginning to sound a little wacky. The invention of the labor-saving device, it has been aptly observed, has killed leisure. Have you ever considered the idea of making life easier for yourself by not buying the extra TVs and machines?

If you won't work overtime, you'll take the other option—a loan. This may start you on a long trip downhill. Taking out loans is easy; banks do their best to make it seem painless. So easy and painless in fact that it quickly becomes a habit, and you dig yourself into a financial hole from which you may never get out.

A loan is merely a postponement of the work you will have to perform to earn the money to buy that machine. Unless you inherit a mint from a long-forgotten aunt, these payments are going to put you in arrears, eat into what little savings you have, and reduce your weekly check. You may have to take out a loan to finance the payments on the first loan. Deeper down you go.

When the installment payments on the various contraptions become too numerous and confusing, you think that you will simplify things by consolidating your debts, and there are always institutions glad to do that for you. That will surely cut down on your postage and checking costs, but it will increase your interest and sink you yet deeper. Unless you are to go bankrupt or run away from it all, you will have to turn to that overtime or moonlighting you thought you were evading by taking the loan option. You have merely postponed the day of judgment.

And now at last you will face the question faced by the man who rather than taking out loans opted for overtime right away—is the work put in worth the work supposedly saved? Only you will be worse off, because he at least, by confronting the overwork imperative head-on, is working for his own money, whereas you, who ducked it by taking out loans, are now working overtime in good part for the banks, paying off interest and interest on interest.

Most Americans are making something like $15,000, but they have had habits instilled into them which only $25,000 or $35,000 can support. That means that many are *working overtime* making money *for the banks* in order to be able to enjoy—enjoy?—the *labor-saving* machines. Good luck, Charley!

The drive to accumulate becomes a bad habit

But even these flies in the ointment are still bearable compared to what follows. Here we come to a peculiarly

American madness: the dependence on technology and devices gets out of hand, the machine-buying habit takes over, and the overtime goes for things that aren't even labor-saving or necessary. When the list of necessaries (or so most of them have come to seem) is exhausted, people continue their buying habits and turn to gadgets that are not only not necessary but foolish.

Take the electric wine-bottle opener. It does not do anything that the manual opener does not do. Yet many feel compelled to buy it simply because it is electric. It has a motor; it makes a noise; it is modern. Depending on your own muscles has come to seem somehow backward and benighted. Or take the recent pet-rock craze. The object in question consists of a rock in a cardboard box and costs five dollars. It does not do *anything*. It has no motor; it makes no noise; but it is modern, and above all it is fashionable. And a strong reason for buying these gimmicks is the need to keep up with others.

People do not appreciate sufficiently how extensive this foolishness is. All one has to do is look at a catalogue from a department store: A crepe maker ($30 for something that turns out to be "a gourmet fry pan"); a Super Shooter cookie gun for $23 (you really mean that your child cannot be persuaded to eat that cookie if it is not shaped like a guided missile and colored in Dayglo?); a pressure cooker (that reduces a two-hour cooking procedure to a half-hour, including takeoff and landing); a microwave oven (that reduces the same operation to a few minutes); a crockery slow cooker (that *increases* the same operation by *many* hours); and on and on it goes.

Are you, then, such a pampered, fragile soul that you must have your crepes done in a "crepe maker" rather than just in a good old $3 frying pan used for lots of other things? There may be a difference in taste, but not three out of a hundred people would be able to discern it *blindfolded*. Are you hovering so near a state of collapse that if all sorts of small appliances were not brought to your rescue, you would be done in?

A case can admittedly be made for the use of every gadget. The question is, however, *do you really need it? Or are you being brainwashed into thinking that you do?*

SEVEN-DAY WONDERS IN THE BASEMENT

For the answer to that, we must examine under the psychological microscope a single item. Let us take wristwatches. Once they merely told time. Now they tell you the time in Rio de Janeiro, Cairo, and Melbourne, and they reflect your moods or put on a color show.

And as if these watches were not good enough as they are, technology comes along with LED and LCD watches. Even if these proved to be slightly more accurate than the old-fashioned ones, one might question their importance. Airline pilots, radio announcers, and a few other kinds of specialty workers need such devices, but for the vast majority of people, the old-fashioned watches are themselves as accurate as is necessary for everyday life.

Even setting that aside, it turns out that these gadgets have serious drawbacks. Some cannot be seen well in daylight. Some need to have batteries checked and to be recalled. Expert repairers sometimes cannot be found or charge high fees. Above all, in a manner that is typical of progress, for something gained, you lose something. It perhaps is helpful to have a number like 12:14 on your watch instead of having momentarily to translate a diagram or angle—as formed by the hands of the conventional watch—into that number (although the number of people who really lose any perceptible time over that translation must be limited to those who cannot walk and chew gum at the same time). Experience has established, however, that the angles of a conventional watch do not merely convey the exact time, as was thought, but also enabled a person to visualize the block of time left before a certain deadline. The new watches, in giving only the present minute and not the face of the entire hour, make it a little more difficult to visualize the block of time left. This may, therefore, be yet another gadget of which you will tire.

People buy gadgets not only because they believe them to be a panacea but also because they notice others doing so. You suspect that you might be missing out on something that your neighbors are into if you do not follow suit. If one person on the block gets a CB radio, pretty soon everyone else feels the pressure—either from within the self or the family—to do the same. One moped begets dozens in a community—or a sailfish, a camper, a swimming pool. No one wants to lose out on a secret of the good life, not even if it costs thousands of dollars.

Next time you are on a spending spree, ask yourself: *how many basements and attics in America are filled with seven-day wonders—new or fashionable things bought in response to an advertising slogan or an impulse?* The question is, Do *you* need this? Will it really make you happier, deep down and permanently, *apart from giving you the transitory pleasure that comes with removing the packaging from some new device, smelling it, taking note of the warranty, and operating it for the first time?*

Save steps

Another reason for buying the gadgets is to make life easier for yourself. But is all physical activity bad? A little advertisement on the envelope from the telephone company is terribly revealing. It says, "Save steps. Get an extension." How typical that is of our time, and how docilely people accept the wisdom of that remark without the slightest question! "Save steps" for what? A telephone extension by itself is not, to be sure, an important item; but as a typical example, as part of a way of life, it is telling. If in every aspect of life you resort to shortcuts of the kind that the telephone extension represents, if you attempt to save labor in every way, what will be the result?

For one thing, your legs and hands may become as atrophied and useless as the appendix. With each step of progress, comes—as a price—a step back. The acceleration of the modern trend toward a sedentary existence, in conjunction with overeating and, particularly, eating "junk" processed foods, leads to obesity and attendant ailments. Running across the house to answer phone calls is not by itself going to put into fine physical shape; all the same, doing that, in conjunction with hundreds of other actions, will make a difference.

We are not exaggerating here. A few years ago, a physician urged people not to buy a remote control (another costly gadget!) for their television sets, because the few trips they make each night between their seats and their sets constitute needed exercise. One can hardly think of a more pathetic sign of how bad off the modern American's physical condition is if he or she must depend on a few walks across the living room for minimal exercise!

Can you imagine people in any other century or land, people dependent on their legs and hands, being so depleted of exercise? How did this happen almost overnight?—because of all the labor-saving devices. And because of the selling job made by the manufacturers and the retailers of them. And because of gullible people who rush out to buy them to "save steps" and save time. *Save for what? For possible obesity, sloth, weakness, physical incompetence.*

The original commendable drive to eliminate back-breaking labor has resulted, by being carried beyond all normal limits, in an elimination of even necessary, stimulating, or limited labor. You may "save steps," all right, but lose your well being.

Many people surround themselves at considerable expense with objects of no lasting merit and of ultimate irrelevance. They mistakenly see accumulation as a source of pleasure. They confuse passing pleasure with ultimate happiness. *They assume that the mere heaping up of things in general and gadgets in particular will buy happiness. The fact is that they will buy comfort, leisure, and convenience, all right, but that these things often have little to do with happiness.* One can be poor and happy, as well as prosperous and miserable.

A psychological diagram and equation

Consider the conclusions of a sage who thought the matter through. The basic human situation, he found, consists of a person and an object. The only relationship between them is that the person desires the object—be it sex, love, beauty, money, power, fame. Contentment is achieved when the object is attained; discontent when it is not.

There are two ways of achieving contentment. Most people go about it in one way, by trying to obtain the object. That is fine—when it works. The trouble is that it often does not work. The object may be unobtainable. You want, for instance, to have a Lincoln Continental or a Mercedes Benz, but you earn $12,000 a year, and there is no

way you can materially increase your salary in the forsee-
able future.

Or the object is obtainable but at too high a price. You
can get that expensive car if you are willing to become involved in illegal activities or to spend all your free time in a
second or third job. But the price you would have to pay is
simply too much for the pleasure of the car.

Or the object is attainable, and you discover it to be
not what you wanted. Or the object is attainable, but with
the passage of time, your tastes—not it—change. And
then it is as if you really did not want the object. You are
back to square one, wanting something you do not have.

The alternative way of operating and—according to
the sage—the better, simpler way is to *stop wanting the object*. That, at first and to most people, seems by far the
more painful and difficult task. Yet it proves *in the long run*
to be the easier thing to do. It requires a lot of introspection and self-discipline, a lot of asking yourself if you really
want or need something.

That this task is not impossible can be readily established by a look at your past. You will recall having at some
period in your life deeply wanted something and felt frus-
trated over not getting it. As a child you wanted an electric
train set or a toy tank, but your parents—because they
could not afford it or because you were naughty—did not
get it; and you were miserable. Yet a year or two later, you
had moved on to other interests, and not having the train
did not matter. So will it happen with your current "toy."

ADJUST YOUR SIGHTS AND SHOP ACCORDINGLY

In childhood and early adulthood, you might have
wanted to be the top ball player, sportscaster, musician,
dancer, lover, boxer, student, runner, prizewinner in the
school and community. As you were growing up and

maturing, you began to separate your fantasies from your accomplishments. You learned to adjust your sights accordingly. And this must hold also for shopping.

The Council for Family Financial Education has developed a list of eleven questions to be asked before buying something. Among them are: "Do you really need this item?"—a question not to be answered glibly; "Is the price reasonable?"—meaning, among other things, within the range of *your* income and your other commitments; "Is this the best time to buy?"—if you are going to buy an air conditioner, for instance, do so when retailers are eager to get rid of excess machines and offer good deals, in August, and not in the middle of the season's first heat wave in early June.

Moderation in the accumulation of things is called for. Some gadgets are materially helpful. Others are not, but you may allow yourself some indulgences. Many others you do not need and should not bother about. As a wise man has said, "Simplify! Simplify!" Little that we have do we need. What we truly possess is not ours but a part of us, inside us. The rest is tinsel, vanity.

King Solomon and the piece of chalk

You can still have what you want, if you learn to reduce your desires. Having something is better than having nothing. There is a story about King Solomon not to be found in either Bible or Bible commentary. As Solomon was applying his renowned wisdom to the problems of his people, one of his numerous children interrupted him with a request for chalk. The king unfortunately found that he had only one long piece in his pocket.

"Oh Dad! My sister wants a piece also!"

"Really?" Solomon said and thought deeply for a

minute. "Here," he finally said as he broke the chalk in two and gave the pieces to the perfectly satisfied boy.

The physicists and economists present at Solomon's court immediately invoked the law of conservation of matter and the law that there are no free lunches, by way of humbly pointing out to His Majesty that his son had been gypped; the boy had asked for more and instead was given back under false pretenses only what he had already possessed.

Solomon replied with a serene, confident smile: "Not at all. If my son had requested two *long* pieces or two ounces, my action would indeed have been deceptive. But he only asked for, and it turned out only wanted, two pieces of chalk. That they were small and weighed only a half-ounce each interfered in no way with his pleasure. In a case like that, the simple expedient of breaking the chalk in two solves the problem."

This solution will obviously not apply in all situations. If a piece of bread and two starving children had been at issue, breaking the bread in half might leave both still somewhat hungry, whereas giving the whole piece to one might sate that one and starve the other. However, other seemingly insoluble problems can, like the one with the chalk, be resolved relatively painlessly with only a little intelligent thought. You might find just as much happiness by *desiring what is obtainable, namely half of what you now desire*. There are many cases where number rather than size or weight matter.

15

Kicking
the
Habit

The habit of habit

"Habit," the Duke of Wellington is supposed to have said,
"is second nature." He meant that some things we do in-
stinctively, such as turning away from too bright a light,
and others we are trained to perform as if they were in-
stinctive, reflex actions. One of the things that distin-
guishes human beings from animals is the role of habit.
The latter are born programmed to do a host of things
that human beings can only gradually learn to do.

Habit therefore means domesticating the wild, making the strange familiar, turning chaos into order; and no
one can deny the vast importance of habit to civilized life
in general and modern life in particular. If you had to confront the act of putting on your clothes and tying your
shoelaces in the morning as though it were a novel
experience—as a child confronts it—you would spend the

better part of the day just on those activities. As a result of habit, these actions are dispatched in a couple of minutes, and you are ready to move on to important functions. They are dispatched so fast, in fact, that you do not even notice them. Habit—training the muscles to perform without engaging the mind—has the important role of freeing the mind for momentous things like the problem of squaring the circle or of solving inflation.

Your habits and those of people working with you ensure that everyone slated to attend a ten o'clock committee meeting or class arrives on time and that the business to be gone through is disposed of promptly. If habit were absent, if one person consequently showed up at 8:30 A.M., another at 11:20 A.M., a third at 2:06 P.M., the class would either never get together or all other classes and work schedules would have to be postponed. Then, during the class or committee meeting, habit is in abeyance as novel experiences are confronted—like learning for the first time of Lincoln's weaknesses as president or of the proposed ad campaign for selling Slop soap—and then habit takes us to the next class or meeting. Habit dictates our attendance at a particular eatery for lunch, the people we eat with and talk to, many of the things we do in the afternoon at school or work, the circumstances attendant on dinner, the particular TV shows we watch each week, the newspapers we read, the late news we watch, the time and manner of our going to sleep. Only in sleep, that is in dreams, do habits disappear; and the world we then enter therefore has a strange surrealist quality. *That world of dreams is precisely what our daily waking lives would be like without the presence of habit.*

Habit is, then, the gradual encroachment of repetition, pattern, and coherence on a universe of randomness, uncertainty, incoherence. Without habit, we could never get beyond $1+1=2$ to algebra, calculus, and particle physics; or from "Mary had a little lamb" to *Hamlet*; truckers could not drive; plumbers could not plumb.

Habit is taking things for granted. We saw in Chapter 8 that all statements rest on certain things that are accepted as true by speaker and auditor, even though no evidence is given for their being true. *These unexamined assumptions are therefore intellectual habits—good habits if the assumptions are valid, bad habits if the assumptions are, or have become with the passage of time, questionable.* Our lives consist of large masses of such mental habits.

The trouble with habit

Clearly, in order to create a better world, we need lots of habit; and often trouble comes from those individuals who—through incompetence, ignorance, rebelliousness—will not adopt habit. *Habit, however, is not everything.* It can become for some people pernicious and does become for many people one of their biggest problems. Like many things in life, habit is indispensable in moderation but harmful in excess. Excess of habit is hardening of the spiritual arteries, both in self and in society.

Habit cuts you off from novelty, raw experience, change—that is, from life itself. Let us say that you are a farmer and your cousin, a lifelong city dweller, comes to visit you for a week's vacation in the summer. Long inured to a world of brick, asphalt, and concrete, your cousin becomes excited over an environment she has not seen in years. "Wow! Look at those beautiful fields, those majestic trees, those imposing mountains, the beautiful brook, the lovely, trusting squirrels; the play of sunlight on bushes and branches and fields, the peaceful cows. Look at the sweet cycles and rhythms of nature, the absence of the rat race, of cars, of discord and tension. What an idyllic existence you lead here, in contrast with mine!"

Your cousin carries on in this emotional manner, because—wrenched from her locale and accustomed way of doing things—she finds everything—which she sees and hears as if for the first time—strange and therefore beautiful. Her eyes and ears are open—as they are not in the city and as yours are not here. To you, she seems naive, sentimental, or bats.

When *you* look at those fields, you don't see beauty; you see rather a harvest of so much wheat or corn this fall, making you so much money. The trees to you are not majestic but a pain because of the trouble you have keeping bugs and blight away from them. The mountains, the birds, the brooks—you stopped noticing you don't know how many years ago. As for the absence of the rat race, did your cousin ever try dealing with the feed suppliers, the farm machinery sellers, the middlemen to whom you deliver the crops, cattle, chickens, and eggs? And what of droughts, floods, tornadoes, untimely frosts, plant and animal diseases, and human thievery?

What has happened? It is a case of the grass being greener on the farmland than on city concrete, of course; but it is also a case of the difference that habit makes. One view is shaped by habit, the other not. Life on the farm means to you doing and seeing things the same way perennially, but to your cousin everything about that life is different, novel. She is, moveover, on vacation, and you are not. *Vacation means no habit.* To her, therefore, everything is magical; to you, tiresome.

Now turn things around. You go to the city to visit your cousin for the first time in several winters. It is your turn to be awed by everything you see, and it is your cousin's turn to look with condescension at you. Your cousin, having been in the city too long, has become jaded, blasé. Habit sees to it that nothing surprises her anymore; nothing shocks or delights.

Who is right and who is wrong? *It is not a question of right or wrong but of where you stand in relation to what you see. And that, in turn, is determined by habit, or its absence.*

Opening yourself to new experiences

No matter what your job may be or where you live, the pattern of work itself will require repetitiveness. Could you function as a farmer if you stared each day at the beauty of field, tree, or mountain? Could your cousin function well as an executive if in walking down the city street every day to work, she gawked at the great buildings rather than meditating on the day's transactions? *This restricted focus is both necessary for vocational health and dangerous for mental health. A secret of life is therefore to achieve a delicate equilibrium, to perform a balancing act with both habit and novelty, order and spontaneity.*

THE NEW ROUTE

How to go about it? Begin with the humblest actions. Look at the way you proceed to and from work: You go along the same streets every day, even the same side of the streets. Everything having become familiar, sights and sounds no longer register along the way. Try a simple experiment tomorrow. Cross the street and proceed along its other side. Better yet, proceed along an alternate route, along adjacent streets. You will be surprised at how much of a change, initially, such a trivial shift in routine can make. Suddenly your environment looks somewhat different. Because of the slight alteration in perspective, you see little things you had not seen before. Although painting has been recommended as a hobby on the grounds that it makes you newly aware of the sheer look of things, a break in routine can do the same with the sights and sounds of everyday life.

Then expand your break in routine. Don't just go down the other side of the street; go by an entirely different route. Try different modes of transport. Switch from car to public transport, or vice versa; from bus to train or subway or the other way around. Try coming in at different times. Try, when taking a bus or train, to skip the morning paper and rather view the world outside your window as though you were a foreigner or a Martian seeing it for the first time. Notice the looks of the buildings, the people, the patterns of residential and suburban and rural structures, the architecture, the stores. Think of the lives lived in those places.

These are, to be sure, small things, but they are a beginning to opening yourself to new experiences. If football, baseball, and basketball are your exclusive viewing choices on TV, venture out of your mental ghetto. Try a slight change—soccer, tennis, or golf. You might be surprised. Then, whether or not that works, go a little further afield. Try news documentaries. Try the Boston Pops. Try drama. Try ballet. You may find that you never really gave that stuff a chance or that when you did, you were too young and naive to know what you were doing.

If that works out, try next going to such affairs in person instead of settling for TV images. You may not like everything at once, but you may like some things enough to want to explore further. Give it a chance; *give yourself a chance.*

There is no right or wrong leisure-time activity. There is no high or low culture. There is no "in" or "out" taste. These are distinctions made by complacent snobs, whether they are aesthetes or hard hats. *There is only open- or closed-mindedness. There is only habit or openness to experience.*

PARALYSIS OF SPONTANEITY

Another ailment caused by overdependence on habit is paralysis of spontaneity. How many people throw down whatever they happen to be doing and betake themselves to a movie or a sunset, to a lecture or a museum, a ball game or a hayride? Acting in that way often, as some do, is bad. It means an absence of commitment or pattern, an inability to focus and function, a life-style without goals. Such people do everything spontaneously, because they have no chart or direction.

But by far the greater danger comes from the many who have too much of a goal. Prisoners of work habits, calendars, watches, lists, and deadlines, they never see their way to doing something unplanned. Should a friend call up and suggest an outing that night, they feel as if all their carefully plotted plans would collapse if they said yes. A movie, a museum visit, or a dinner date must be planned weeks in advance. Even the spontaneous act must take its place in a sequence of planned, coherent actions.

What such people, sometimes called "workaholics," suffer from is terminal stages of Habititis. Their lives have been mortgaged away to schedules and routine. Spontaneous outbursts have long since been squelched or deflected into harmless brief acts like eating a peach out of turn. Even scheduled holidays and days off, though ostensibly vacations from work, have long since been sold into the bondage of plans and itineraries.

Delight in the unforeseen

Think of the delight caused when an unforecast snowstorm sneaks into the city at night and you wake up in the morning to find three feet of snow on the ground and a free day on your hands.

THE LABELING HABIT

Nor should you neglect to take a vacation from those habits of belief we call values. You have to stop being so quick to judge. In looking at anything, don't rush to label it "good" or "evil," "right" or "wrong." Look, for a change, at events under the aspect of eternity. In that way, the sheer scope of something and not whether it was good or bad is paramount. In an Olympic competition, we admire the athletes' deeds without asking whether they cheat on their love partners or tax returns. Life becomes more fascinating and mysterious in that way. To repeat to oneself and to others during a performance of Shakespeare's *Richard III* or *Othello* that a particular character is a villain is to make a bore of oneself as well as to miss the point of the play. The fact of villainy is established clearly at the very beginning, so that one can turn to other, more interesting matters.

Don't miss the point

There is nothing immoral about suspending judgments. Scientists do it all the time in order to understand the universe around them. For you to do so is to bring the rigors of scientific inquiry to other fields. In reading about other cultures, individuals, and religions, bringing your own values to bear has its uses, albeit only within limits. You will never understand these other individuals and groups unless you learn to see them on their own terms and to put yourself into their shoes.

THE COST OF LIVING

Another habit is judging by money. Many people think of everything in terms of how much it will make or cost. Athletes, for instance, are now known mainly in terms of how large their salaries are and how long their contracts. Assessing all things in terms of numbers with dollar signs in front of them is to forget that financial value is no indication of absolute worth but only of the current fetching price. A good thing may be ubiquitous and therefore cheap, but still a good thing. When the crop is good, there is hardly a fruit as luscious as a sugar plum, and when the crop is large, it is to be had inexpensively; but no one would maintain that the fruit does not taste good simply because it is cheap. Conversely, when the crop is bad, the fruit will be high priced but uninspiring in taste.

Many of life's delights—sunsets, zoos, concerts, books—are experiences to be had for little or nothing. They are therefore ignored by the money-oriented crowds. When the Metropolitan Museum of Art in the early 1960s purchased Rembrandt's *Aristotle Contemplating the Bust of Homer* for a record-setting sum in the millions, there was a huge outpouring of gallery-goers. The room in which the painting was on exhibit had to be kept open late while the rest of the museum was closed. Clearly there was no overnight upsurge of interest in art. What people were going to see was not art, not Rembrandt, certainly not Aristotle or Homer, but *money*. They came to look at a display of $2 million in the form of a painting, and most of them went away having seen nothing more than money.

SURPRISE YOURSELF

Perhaps some were bestirred enough to visit the other wings of the museum, to become interested in Rembrandt's etchings, to look up Aristotle in the encyclopedia, or to read Homer's *Iliad*. These few people allowed an experience to break through their habits. They learned to stop thinking only about dollar signs and numbers. They learned to begin thinking. Perhaps to their own surprise, they discovered the realm of art, the world of philosophy, or the pleasures of literature, for those things were also on display. *You can be among those happy few.*

THE IGNORANCE OF THE SPECIALIST

Habit also explains the special ignorance of the specialist, the person who responds to events in the manner for which he or she was trained—sometimes three or four decades earlier—and has allowed that manner to settle, rather as some houses settle into their foundations, awkwardly at an angle. No use pointing out that technology has marched forward, assumptions have replaced each other, that the very methods of research have altered. Since degrees and diplomas are awarded for life, physicians can go through the decades, blithely misdiagnosing patients because of their habituated adherence to the training and to the ideas that reigned long ago. The average expert in any field is actually as much a victim of habit as the nonspecialized, nonexpert manual laborer—perhaps even much more so. That expert often exhibits consequently an ignorance that is subtle and sometimes profoundly expensive—and in lives, not just money.

Break the habit

Habit is, then, a central human experience. It tames the chaos we are born into and domesticates a world otherwise mysterious. When people make an inference or generalization, they impose on life a semblance of coherence. When they revisit or reuse that generalization, they establish a habit. Such an island of light in the midst of the vast darkness is precious to us. Standing alone between humanity and chaos, this rampart becomes a vested interest of ours. It is, though, a blessing that can turn into a curse; a crutch that can help and then hinder.

To treat this ailment, you must take heavy doses of novelty and an injection of spontaneity. Change your perspective frequently, and ventilate your assumptions. A periodic logical checkup and psychological self-examination is also necessary. Cure yourself of this habititis before it becomes a terminal illness. Rid yourself of this, the biggest of the hurdles in your head.

IV

It's Time to Live

Now that the deck has been cleared of pseudoideas and negative ideas, you are ready to consider a plan of action, an offensive — not a mere excursion — into the realm of living. Your logic is beginning to stand on its own feet, your common sense is blossoming, your voracious conscience has been confined to the definite but limited province that is its own by right. At long last, these measures of resuscitation are making palpable the pulse of your ego. Get up and enter life, enter your very own life. Look to your body, your values, your actions.

The ways of doing so are simple and obvious, so much so that you will wonder why you had not thought of them before on your own. You forget that they are obvious only after the veils of illusion and confusion *have been removed from your eyes. Before that inner liberation, nothing was simple or clear; everything seemed impossible or difficult. Only remove the roadblocks you ran into, and then watch the horizons broaden, the opportunities multiply.*

The specific measures for change are: freeing yourself from the wearying passive wait for something to turn up and so taking your own fate into your own hands and carving a more satisfying identity for yourself; freeing yourself from the slavery that con-sumes time; freeing yourself from the slavery to the past and to the future so as to be free for the elusive present—which is the only time you have—*brief and precious as it is. Then you are ready for the leap into life.*

16

Waiting for Lightning to Strike

Only failure is guaranteed

A counselor at a certain school often urges his students to apply for the various scholarships and grants offered by organizations like the Ford Foundation and the Police Athletic League. Most students, not feeling sufficiently endowed with the creative selfishness that we have been stressing throughout this book, respond with a diffident, "Who me?"—as if scholarships were made for Einsteins, astronauts, and athletes only. Then they launch into a predictable series of self-deprecatory statements: "I'm really not very brilliant"; "My school record is not good enough"; "My teachers won't recommend me"; "The odds are against me because so many people are applying"; "I belong to the wrong sex (or ethnic) group"; "My name begins with the wrong initial"; "The astrological charts are not favorable."

The counselor listens to all this with a wry smile. Then, when he is sure that every last drop of self-distrust is out of the system, he sends out his short but powerful rejoinder: "Well, I cannot guarantee that if you apply for the scholarship you will get it. But in this uncertain life, the one thing I *can* guarantee is that if you *don't* apply, you *won't* get it."

This may sound like a wise-guy statement, a polite way of urging someone to stop griping and get on with the task. It is that, of course, but it is also a profound observation on how we barricade ourselves against helpful incursions of reality and take measures to prevent anything from improving our conditions. Our inertia is so powerful that it will force us to think up any nonsense to avoid doing what will aid us.

Of excuses, there is never any shortage. Even if these have some substance to them, in most cases they will play a small role in determining whether or not the applicant will obtain the scholarship. The way to get the scholarship is to ask for it. The way to improve your condition is to do something. Instead of trying to prove how a new idea won't work, one would be better advised to study how to make it work. Instead of thinking up all the reasons why you might not get the scholarship, it is far better to put your energy and time into thinking up a project good enough to overcome all the objections you raise.

The Messiah watch

But that would require getting off our behinds and doing something, anything. Most of us prefer to wait. To wait for lightning to strike. To wait for Lefty. To wait for Godot. To wait for the fix. To wait for Fortuna.

THE POLITICAL MESSIAH

We wait, some of us, for Lefty—for the political messiah, for the revolution, for the right president and party to get into the White House, turn the rascals out, and reorganize society. In the political utopia that is just around the corner, that will come into being if the politician that we work for is elected, employers will come begging us to take jobs and go to work for them at high salaries.

THE RELIGIOUS MESSIAH

We wait, others among us, for Godot—for the religious messiah, for the coming of a spiritual utopia where people will stop competing with each other (especially *they* with *me*), and where everyone will recognize the spiritual worth of the other guy, mostly *they* of *mine*.

THE PERFECT FIX

Or we wait for the perfect fix—for the ultimate marijuana from Mexico or Colombia, poppy from Turkey, LSD from some college lab, booze from Seagram's. It will send us off into a long-lived "high" from which we will rarely have to return to such sordid realities as doing the dishes, sorting out the laundry, making out tax forms, asking someone out for a date, studying for exams, or telling someone off.

Lightning is not going to strike

The only trouble is that lightning won't strike. It's got so much ground to cover, it won't get around to you. You might as well wait to win the lottery. It is possible that you might be lucky, but to plan for that great day when you win a million dollars is silly. Even when months of weekly or daily lottery-ticket purchases go by without any results, some people tell themselves, "Oh boy, my number must be coming up now. Just by the law of averages. I've lost so many times that I'm going to win any day now."

The trouble with the lottery and that kind of thinking, of course, is that it's only another dodge, another excuse to do nothing with your life. Instead of waiting for Lefty or for Godot, it is waiting for Fortuna—the goddess of Chance, Fate, Fortune, Luck, Breaks. Sometimes, people indeed get touched in the shoulder or forehead by her, and they are automatically sent into a different and presumably better orbit. Most of us, however, just get to throw away the losing lottery ticket. Another week and another $1 or $5 gone down the drain. Another week wasted moaning over that haughty goddess, Fortuna. Another week's postponement of getting down to work and confronting oneself.

THE TROUBLE WITH LIGHTNING STRIKING

If you really want to get straightened away, put aside these pipe dreams about Lefty, Godot, or Fortuna. The messiah may very well come, *though whether for better or worse, no one knows.* Fortuna may very well touch you, but whether for good or ill, you don't know and may not want to know.

Fortuna is, after all, connected not only with good things like lottery winnings but also with bad things like heart attacks and automobile accidents. Sometimes the lightning you may get hit by is not figurative but literal, and the results of that are painful, not pleasant. When you think of the many ways in which Fortuna can affect you, the unpleasant ones may be more numerous than the pleasant ones. You are *statistically more likely to get a traffic ticket than a winning lottery ticket*. So maybe, on thinking it over, you will wisely conclude that the less business you have with old Miss Fortuna, the better.

Doing rather than waiting

What choices are you then left with? What can you do with your life? Plenty, once you eliminate the pipe dreams and the flimflam picked up from advertising, propaganda, and Hollywood.

You must realize that up to a point, you can make your own luck, if you then still want to call it "luck." There are, of course, people who work hard at something for years and then have nothing to show for it—no expected breakthrough, no great discovery or victory. Or they achieve the hoped-for result, only to have it destroyed by bad luck. About such things, little can be done. But such reversals occur only to some people. These constitute as small a minority as those who sit around doing nothing and are struck by good luck.

GROWING UP

In the middle is the large mass of people who, if they work hard at something, with average intelligence and foresight, will have something to show for the commitment. So it's up to you to get going and join that large majority. There is no pot of gold at the end of the rainbow unless you yourself put it there. You have to make your own luck; anything else is childish.

Children have things done for them. When they are very young, every need of theirs is attended to. As they grow older, they take over more and more of those tasks until at maturity, they do virtually everything for themselves and even quite a bit for others. That is the way it remains through the long decades of adulthood and maturity.

To depend on others, in this case Fortuna, to do things for you and to bring you gifts is therefore a form of childishness, a sign of not being grown-up emotionally. To be an adult means not asking for guarantees that if you do anything, your effort will be crowned by success or not foiled by Fortuna. But in either case, the counselor's advice is to the point. Whether you will achieve anything or not is not clear; if you *do* try you *may* not get it. But if you *don't* try, you *certainly* won't get it.

Free will

The matter is like free will in philosophy. Most theologians insist on the paradox that we have free will. Some people say that if God is all-powerful and all-knowing, we lack free will. Others claim that all behavior is determined by biology, chemistry, economics, etc. To all this theorizing, there is only one simple answer: It doesn't matter whether we in fact have free will, for that's a theoretical question. What matters is the practical level; and if you feel that you have a choice between two courses of action, you have free will. Even if our actions are predestined, as long as we don't know in what manner they are predestined and what course they are to take, it is as if we had free will. So act, and you may succeed.

Starting now

Getting that job

What does all this mean in practical terms? Here's a concrete example. Are you just out of school and finding it hard to get a job? There are few openings in the field? Don't just sit there complaining to your friends and relatives. There are bound to be some job openings from time to time. Even in the worst labor markets, there is a turnover as people retire, move on, or are fired. Sit right down, therefore, and start typing out that résumé. Write to all the companies and employment agencies. Talk to people and make phone calls. Look up old, or set up new, contacts. Use your time to drop in on some companies in the area.

Who knows? Few as the openings are, you just might happen to be writing a letter, making a phone call, or dropping in at the moment when a vacancy occurs. Although they may have files and long lists of people waiting to be tapped, if you happen to be around at the right juncture, they would rather take you than start the tedious process of going through dusty files and telephoning people.

Don't become discouraged

Knock on every door. Expect setbacks. Welcome them, relish them, savor them. Make them familiars, not strangers, and they can't hurt you. When they come, you'll react like the movie character who continues walking unflinchingly as the bullets hit his body.

There's always the next day. Face things realistically. Stop fantasizing, or leave it for sleeping hours only. Keep up your efforts. Think of the years Michelangelo had to

195

put in on the Sistine Chapel ceiling, and most of that was spent in an awkward position with neck strained and back aching, in sweltering heat in the summer. Or think of the years Tolstoy had to work on *War and Peace*, which is 1,500 pages long and weighs a few pounds. You, by contrast, have it easy.

IMPROVING YOUR SOCIAL LIFE

So too with your social life. Stop waiting for lightning to strike. Stop sitting around, expecting the phone to ring. Start doing things. Go where other single people congregate. This may mean going to singles' weekends and school reunions, joining organizations. You will not like everyone you meet. But you never know when you may run into somebody on your wavelength. For all you know, after nine wasted sessions, there will come one meaningful one—one that will more than make up for all the wasted ones.

Try skiing and après-ski. Try beach resorts, try computer dating. Sure they're silly and rigged, but some do work out, even if only by chance and not by computer wisdom. Join the American Youth Hostel or the Sierra Club, and go on their weekly hikes. Even if nothing happens to you socially, at least you'll get some fresh air into your lungs, some muscles into your legs, and another expertise into your repertory while shaking off your city mustiness.

Call up friends and acquaintances. Call up for dates. If you're female, free yourself from the silly convention that men are supposed to do all the calling. Take your destiny into your own hands, and call the guy up. What are you afraid of? That he'll say no? So what: Let him say no! That's the very worst that can possibly happen to you, and it's not the end of the world.

If you feel that you are not an interesting person because your education is deficient, this is not an insoluble problem. Go to forums, join discussion groups, attend lectures and museums. You don't have to completely like everything you do—though you should choose those things that interest you and that you can read up on. The point is to make yourself visible, make yourself at least interesting. The point is to do something with yourself.

Choose books or lectures on history, philosophy, Greek tragedy, film, psychology, accounting, or politics—*any*thing that will do something for your mind. At the least, it'll give you something to talk about at the next social gathering and make people want to invite you. At the most, it'll give you something to mull over, something positive to do besides brooding over your fate. It'll take you out of yourself. It'll give you the beginnings of an expertise, a way of forging an identity for yourself.

Make your own life-style

There is no easy answer to the question of whether one should concentrate on one activity or go in for varied ones. The answer depends on your situation. Some people concentrate all their energy on one thing—be it sports or politics—and are successes at it, enjoy themselves thoroughly, and lead fulfilled lives.

Other people prefer variety. Although successful as lawyers, they need also to write historical novels and play superlative tennis. Here again, as long as they enjoy their diversified life-styles, they—although choosing an approach very different from the monomaniacs—are as psychically well off as the others.

The problem is therefore not with the life-style but

with the life-styler. Any life-style can satisfy some person—and by the same token can dissatisfy another. You begin by finding out where you are happy and where unhappy. You may be spreading yourself too thin, or you may be too absorbed in one thing at the expense of others.

But most people are probably too monomaniacal. They do not explore themselves and their capacities. If you are one of them, don't forget that it is important to have various irons on the fire—partly by way of finding yourself, partly so that when rebuffed, you fall back on the other things you are banking on.

In the same way, if you are a compulsive list maker and rigid planner and your work habits lead to achievement and success, stick to your lists and plans. If they do not, try change, try improvisation, playing it by ear. You may find that that works better, that your fear of relying on memory, chance, and impulse is exaggerated. On the other hand, if you operate on memory, impulse, and the like and you are having trouble coping, try making lists and plans for a change; try imposing a schedule or routine on yourself. You may find that that organizes your thought and achieves results. If it does not, you can always go back to your old work habits.

Nor can anyone presume to tell you how to resolve the choice faced by the ancient hero Achilles: whether to live a long life in obscurity or a short, intense life of deeds and fame. This is your decision. The important thing is to do. Do lots of things, and they will make things happen, either by themselves or in connection with each other. *Instead of waiting for lightning to strike, generate your own electricity.*

17

Killing Time Is Murder

Lack of time

The reader who has journeyed with us this far but is hesitating over commitment will probably now say, "Yes, yes, yes. It all makes sense, and I'm really going to change my life this time. Only not just now, but tomorrow . . . or a few days from now."

"Next week," as the old cartoon had it, "we've got to get organized." "Tomorrow," as a sign in a tavern in a small Irish village says, "all drinks are free." Yet next week and tomorrow easily become the pot of gold at the end of the rainbow. What keeps you from taking that big leap right now, today?

"I've got no time. I'm always so busy."

Always busy? If true, that *is* a major obstacle to overhauling yourself. Anyone without time obviously can't attend to him- or herself, to hang-ups, to bad habits. But wait a moment! If you found the time to analyze with us some of your problems, you surely can find the time to do something about them. Not to do so would be like peeling potatoes and then throwing the potatoes away with the peels.

Unless it turns out that lack of time is precisely one of those problems. Or, more likely, that thinking you have no time is a major problem of yours. We are, after all, living in an age of leisure or, at any rate, an age devoted to turning out ever greater numbers of labor-saving devices. With so much labor being saved, how can you not have time? Are you perhaps fooling yourself? *Is it really lack of time that is bothering you or reluctance to look at yourself, to change your ways?* When your car starts to act up, you quickly find the time to get to a mechanic; when your body hurts in some way, you manage to get to the doctor soon enough. *Is your body or even your car worth more to you than your mind, your happiness?*

"But," you demand to know, "where can I find time? I've got only twenty-four hours a day, labor-saving devices or not. Show me how I can change anything in, or add anything to, my already busy schedule. I know I can't."

A TYPICAL DAY

Very well. But before we can change anything, we must know what the status quo is. Here is how an average American spends the day.

Up at 7. Some half to three quarters of an hour spent on showering, selecting clothes, shaving or cosmeticizing oneself. Breakfast, including a cursory reading of a newspaper, takes a half hour. Transportation, door to door, is worth a good hour at least. The office is reached around 9:30. Then, except for a quarter-hour coffee break, work until 12:30 P.M. Lunch takes an hour. Then work to 5 P.M.

The trip home, with some shopping of incidentals, takes until 6:30. Then dinner and helping wash the dishes. At 7:45 or 8 begins the reading of the afternoon newspaper, as well as continuing with this week's issue of *Newsweek* or *McCall's* or *Sports Illustrated*. That's good for 9 or 9:30. Now come two hours of television viewing. Then to bed.

Or one does not go home from work at all but eats and goes to an evening college course. Or it's a trip, whether alone, on a date, or with the buddies, to a movie, a bowling alley, with homecoming at midnight.

Weekends are more varied, yet often turn out to have a recurring pattern. Saturdays are for shopping—food for the week, clothes for the season, tools and furniture for the years. If not shopping, then cleaning the house, fixing, puttering about; mowing the lawn, raking the leaves, winterizing doors and windows. Sundays it's time for a party, a visit to relatives, a get-together with friends, or an outing. Sunday night, more TV.

All this, the typical American week, hardly leaves time even for reading the current best-seller. So where is one to make room for any new departures like yoga exercises, meditations, stamp collecting, self-improvement? As anyone can see, the problem of time is no small one.

IS EVERYTHING OF EQUAL IMPORTANCE?

No small problem? That depends on how you look at it. If everything continues as it does, you certainly are bogged down in a busy life. That "if," however, is a big assumption. It covers a series of assumptions, namely that everything you do is of equal importance.

Someone defined New York City as a place where people think important things are happening all the time but where in fact nothing ever happens. So is it with most people's lives. *People think that they must continue to do the things they do because they are important or are part of an optimal life-style.*

Many routines are indeed necessary. You have to go to work or school, and it is important to socialize, to keep up with friends; but how important is watching television for two or three hours every night? How important are some other time-consuming activities?

Time for riding and reading

Let's take the most difficult first. Who says that you must spend nearly an hour going each way to work or college? We all know about the modern city, the automobile, the creaky mass-transit situation, the decay of center city, the sociological situation that drives people willy-nilly into the suburbs. But have you examined your own situation to make sure that you are over an hour away from place of work or study because you really have no choice? Or is it only because: (a) it just happened that way, (b) you're doing what everyone else in your crowd is doing, (c) you're too lazy to change anything?

Look at the manner in which four other people have answered that question. Rick Parkins worked for the Abey See Corp. in Manhattan and lived in Queens. Commuting took him forty minutes door to door. Then the company, joining the flight to suburbia, moved to Westchester County. Now commuting consumed more like an hour and a half each way. For three years, Rick fretted and fumed during his daily trips to work. One day, after a talk with a friend who spent all of five minutes driving to work each day, Rick calculated the number of hours of his life he was offering as sacrifice to the great god Commuting. That did it. He cut down on some of his luxury expenses, concentrated on his savings account rather than on speculative stocks, and started studying the classified ads on houses and apartments. Two years later, he moved to a place almost across the street from the firm. The monthly payments for his domicile are somewhat higher, but when Rick thinks of the hours of tedium and rush-hour jams he has excised from his life, he can only sing.

Then there is the case of Holly Alexander, college student. She can't afford the dorm at school, so she has to put in an hour each way, four days a week to get to her Palisades College. Why? Because her best friends in high school were impressed by the school's art program. But a funny thing happened to her on the way through her sophomore year. (a) She has made a new circle of friends and no longer sees much of her high school chums. (b) She has discovered that she wants to be a registered nurse, not a ballerina or sculptress. Her latest boy friend asked, "So why are you dragging yourself all the way to Palisades College?" Result: She now attends her neighborhood college, minutes away.

Simon Epstein reasoned that if the mountain won't come to Mohammed, Mohammed might go to the mountain. Finding, after self-examination, that the pressures that took him to suburbia were too big to overcome, he decided to take another look at the question of whether he must continue to work in the city. At first the idea of switching jobs seemed impossible, but with plenty of self-examination and looking around, "impossible" became a mere "uncomfortable." Switching jobs would involve having to go through his desk (hours of work) and a cut in pay, the same job paying less in the suburbs than in the city.

Then he asked himself whether a reduction of his annual salary from $20,000 to $17,000 was not worth a reduction of travel time one way from one hour to only about ten minutes.

Simon assumed that the answer was "no"—until he actually bothered to do the numbers. A saving of fifty minutes one way, he discovered, is one hour and forty minutes a day; more than eight hours a work week; more than sixteen 24-hour periods in the course of a year or fifty entire workdays; that is, more than *two months of 8-hour workdays a year*! He switched jobs.

At first he thought that he would devote the free time to free-lance work, which would easily make up the $3,000 differential. But then he found he would much rather use the time to begin to find himself. His peace of mind and more leisurely life-style now, in other words, were worth $3,000 to him. For one thing, the less pressured life made him feel that he could do without going to a shrink, so he got his $3,000 back right there. He is sure glad he finally questioned a lot of unexamined assumptions and made the switch.

Is the news hot?

Clarissa Johnson's problem was not commuting—she dormed at the school—but newspapers and magazines. She was having difficulties graduating, because although a senior, she could not force herself to get down to her thesis. She could not resist reading the morning *New York Times* page by page. She could not go to the toilet without a *Time* or *Newsweek*, and that was good for another hour. Sundays were a dead loss to the Sunday *Times*. Friends asked her if she really was writing a dissertation on current

events, if she thought that when she died, St. Peter was
going to give her a ten-hour exam on what happened in
the world while she was alive.

Finally she went to her advisor, who helped her work
it out. "Newspapers," he pointed out, "contain, for the
most part, trivia. Isn't it proverbial that nothing is as dead
as yesterday's newspapers? Besides, do you really keep
posted on important matters or spend most of the time on
the sports pages, the stock market, the gossip columns, and
the prejudices of the political columnist who says just what
you want to hear?

"How then can you justify having spent a couple of
hours yesterday, *a pair of precious hours of your life*, on something that a mere day later is irrelevant? And are you
going to perpetrate the same idiocy today? And again tomorrow?"

"But how can I be a good citizen? How can I vote in-
telligently? Don't I have to know what's going on?"

"No one says that you have to cut yourself off from
events. *Only that you should distance yourself from them.* An occasional reading of a newsmagazine or of the 'Week in Review' section of the Sunday *Times* will fill you in on things.
More than that you don't need, unless you're a professor
of modern history.

"What difference does it make that there is a rent strike
in the Bronx, a mugging in Washington, an indicted judge
in St. Louis, an arrest for cocaine in Berkeley, an election
in Sioux City? You read about the same events a week or a
month earlier; and only because the names of the participants and of the locales are different, you don't recognize
the story. Would you reread the short stories of the world's
greatest writer that many times? Once you've read about
one mugging or indictment, you've more or less read

about all of them. *Except for a few times each decade, when there is hard news, such as the end of a world war or the assassination of a president, the newspapers of any day could be exchanged with the papers of any other day, and it wouldn't make any difference to anybody.*

"So stop wasting as much as two hours every day— *fourteen hours a week*—as well as a good part of Sunday, on newspapers. It's a slavery that's in the head, a mind-forged manacle, a rope of sand. It's a useless habit that, after a brief cold-turkey period, is easily broken."

It took some doing, but Clarissa finally got the message, cut down on newspaper reading, and wrote her thesis.

A TV guide

Some people's Waterloo is neither commuting nor newspapering but TV viewing. That can cost them as much as fifteen to twenty hours a week.

Breaking that televiewing habit at first sounds like major psychic surgery. Let's face it, though; ninety percent of what you are watching is less than ecstasy producing, and you know it. You sit there only because you are too lazy or tired or habituated to it to do anything else. You feel vaguely guilty about it, but you keep on expecting something really good to show up at any minute, even though you know that it won't. What keeps you glued to the set? Nothing, really.

Television is downright harmful in some ways. It disrupts close family ties. It lulls children into passivity and makes them early and trained consumers. Even for adults, it is injurious. Too many people, having to choose between a get-together with friends and acquaintances or a movie on TV, will choose the latter. They will opt for vicarious experience, however dramatic or melodramatic, rather than for human contacts, live conversation, direct concrete personal experience.

TV is deleterious in another important way. Proffering experience at second hand, it distorts our sense of reality. As a comedian put it, when an eclipse of the moon takes place nowadays, we do not watch the eclipsed moon itself, we watch it as shown on the TV news. Things have reached the point where something is not real or true until it has been reported on TV.

The social consequences are dreary to contemplate. On TV shows, the police always catch the killer, the handsome hero and the beautiful heroine always walk off together into the sunset, people are good or bad, and the bad guys—after thriving mightily—get theirs in the end.

Here is a little exercise you might try one night—like tonight. Just say, aloud if necessary, "Who needs this?" Then get up and turn off the set. At once, a deafening silence and a rush of loneliness will overwhelm you.

But hold on; don't panic! Don't rush to the neighbor or worse, to the phone. Some people easily fall into the lulling arms of the telephone and proceed to fritter away many hours there. These vices dutifully pinch-hit for each other if you let them. Instead, you must use the time to make a fresh start in life, to seek a new avocation, to devote yourself to yourself.

A mental diet

No one should infer from this exercise that we recommend such drastic steps as immediate cessation of all TV viewing and newspaper reading. Most people are hardly that athletic or ascetic, nor need they be. We have merely sketched the extreme in order to reveal *how much time you could really accumulate if your life depended on it, how free you really are once you break the unexamined assumptions about commuting, TV, newspapers; how much treasure*—for that is what time is, the supreme treasure, in fact—*is actually lying within your grasp.*

What you can do is go part of the way. You need not choke off all TV viewing. Merely reduce it—how far depends on your sense of crisis. *The stronger your desire to alter your life, the more you should provide the time in which to do something about it.*

You can go about it, as you can go about weight-reducing diets, in various ways. One is cold turkey: Do without TV for a week or two or three in order to prove to yourself how independent of it you can become. Then resume only limited TV viewing. Another way is to reduce it gradually, quitting an hour the first week, two the next, etc. A third way, perhaps in conjunction with the others, is to turn oneself from a passive into a selective viewer. Stop sitting down with the determination to watch something, *any*thing, and flipping the channel selector to find the most appealing show. Instead, go through the week's schedule in the Sunday press supplements, and check off only those programs that sound truly—or relatively—interesting. By way of helping your TV-reducing diet, you might rigidly limit yourself to only an hour or a half hour of nightly viewing. Then stick to your schedule. At all other times, don't go slumming by turning the dial; just turn that set off, and take the plug out of the wall socket if necessary.

TIME FOR A CHANGE

Do you see now how flimsy is the lament of many people, "I never have any time"? Some people not interested in getting out of a rut, afraid to do something about the dissatisfaction with their lives, use this refrain as an excuse for inaction.

You must impose standards on yourself, and throw away those things that do not come up to your standards. You can't passively allow the world to affect and shape you. You have to ask yourself if you really enjoy this, want this, need this. If the answer is unclear, it's time to try something else. It's time, as the political slogan has it, for a change. And the realization that it's time for a change will give you the time in which to make that change, the space in which to find yourself.

Speed-reading and speed-living

Devoting yourself to trivia is not the only way to kill time. Saving time can, ironically, be equally pernicious. *It all depends on what you save time from and for.* "Learn to read an entire novel in a half hour," says the commercial for a speed-reading school. Sounds like good advice? Not so at all! Speed-reading is an excellent tool for getting through multivolumed government or business reports and for reading the Sunday *New York Times* page by page. For reading a novel—be it a classic, a best-seller, or a suspense story—speed-reading is pointless.

Do you need all this speed?

Such books are not read for the absorption of facts but for the stimulation and exercise of the emotions. Fear, suspense, mystery, jealousy, love, regret, awe, excitement, hate, pity—these feelings need elbow room, that is, time in which to expand and bestir themselves. They cannot be cramped into a half-hour cubicle or concentrated into a bouillon cube or vitamin pill. They are, in some enigmatic fashion, a source of joy, and who wants to curtail joy?

SPEED UP THE FILM

Why stop with reducing a novel to a half hour? Why not reduce a full-length film from one and a half or two hours to fifteen minutes, either by accelerating the projection speed or by showing only highlights? Why not also speed-sleep, speed-sex, and speed-anything-that-is-pleasant? Why not speed-living—rushing through life itself? Sounds silly? *But that is exactly the effect you create in your life by racing—reducing the length and enjoyment—through all pleasures. Why not, while you are at it, take all the joy out of life?* After all, it is saving time you are after, and who wants to waste it on poor things like good food, sex, feelings?

The point is that you can *kill time not only by wasting it on trivia but also by speeding up essentials.* By cutting down the time spent on joy, you excise from time all pleasurable experience. To make good use of time is to allow pleasant experiences to occupy it—and you.

Speed-reading militates against the emotions and reflections attendant on leisurely, sensitive reading. Those who read everything, including literature, for facts dismiss such reflective reading as self-indulgence and mushiness. They are wrong. They do not realize that the mental life consists not only of facts and figures, profit and loss, but also of imagination, fantasy, feelings.

A VACATION FROM HABIT

We would go further and defend even the importance of daydreaming, of thinking not attached to any book or real event and not structured in any way. Psychologists have often remarked on the importance of daydreams. Too many of us unfortunately obey the injunction, "Don't just sit there—do something!"

Psychologists also remind us that work itself—make-work, keeping busy—can be an effective form of escape. People who bury themselves in the office from 8 to 8 and on weekends may be fleeing from the need to confront other human beings socially or even to confront their own families. Perhaps a little time off from work would do them good. And one informal, brief, time off is the daydream, which can be carried on right there at the desk. Letting your imagination rove makes you feel better about yourself and, in some curious ways, enriches you. Daydreams are, after all, the sources of the artist's—writer, painter, musician—inspiration, and all of us can be our own artists, up to a point.

Daydreaming is simply a recreation of the world around you, a making of a new world. To only daydream would be as wrong as only working, but to exclude it is no less wrong. Children are born with fine—that is, unregimented—imaginations, but upbringing squelches most of it. Daydreaming is a vacation from habit and a healthy harking back to the spontaneity of childhood.

Be a juggler

There is a seeming contradiction here. On one hand, we emphasize that time is precious and that you may be wasting it on mental junk food when you should be serious and busy. Yet at the same time we say that people take too driven, commercial, efficiency-oriented views of time, that they are in the bad habit of saying, and believing, that time is money and deadlines should be set and met. Along these lines, we would seem to be urging you to adopt a more leisurely, tolerant attitude.

Which is it then to be? Paradox or not, we would have you do *both*, in a sort of juggling act. Be more activist *and* more leisure oriented. Disorganized people leave their lives in a sort of limbo, neither relaxing and enjoying themselves nor accomplishing much. Organized individuals arrange their lives in such a way that they spend their time constructively but simultaneously in an enjoyable way.

Downtown

Take a simple thing like errands. Many people do things piecemeal. They go downtown one day to purchase some clothing. A day or two later, they go downtown to buy records. A day or two after that, a dentist's appointment sends them downtown again. Then there are other errands. This is terribly wasteful.

Far better would it be to arrange your appointments and commitments so that you can bunch them up in one day. Set aside one day a week or a month for taking care of all your downtown chores. Give yourself enough time between chores so that you do not have to rush; attend to them in the order in which they lie geographically. In that way, you will have numerous days free for yourself and a gradual accumulation of things to attend to on your relatively rare outing.

That day downtown will, moreover, take on more of an air of excitement and adventure, partly because it will be relatively rare and partly because it will see many things being attended to. Above all, when you return at the end of that day, you will be very tired but very happy, because you will be able to say to yourself or to your family, "Boy, did I accomplish a lot today!" That is one of life's better moments. Whereas now, you kill a whole day to do one thing downtown and say, "Boy, I wonder where that day went? I hardly accomplished anything today." And, of course, your other days will be free for you to turn to the things that really matter.

What you are doing wrong, then, is taking too much time for incidentals like commuting, TV, newspapers and too little for the stuff of life. Save time from distractions in order to lavish it on fundamentals, in order to wallow in living.

18

The Present
Is
an Instant

Living in the present

Few people know the supreme joy, that of shaping their
own lives. They always think that someone else is doing it,
that their own existence is limited by this person or that
force. Life seems to be a succession of crises and unfore-
seen expenses. Things usually happen to them.

The secret is that to control one's life, one must *live in
the present*. That sounds obvious enough but happens to be
a difficult thing to do. For one thing, the present is so
short; it is less than an instant. The minute that you say
"now," the present has become the past. It is harder to
focus on the present than on a microbe without a microscope.

Another reason is that the mind is, partly by nature
and mainly by conditioning, oriented to the past and the

future. Anything rather than the present. In older, traditional societies, the past looms large; how people did things in earlier times matters greatly. In modern technological societies, people look forward, eagerly expecting to have things better at some time to come.

Individuals behave in this matter like societies, albeit for different reasons. What has been said of some people's appearance applies to the thought processes of people: They spend the first twenty years of their lives trying to look older and the next twenty years trying to look younger.

In other words, no matter what the age, some people try to pass themselves off, as much to themselves as to others, as something other than what they are. So do we all do anything but accept where we are—in the present. As the poet says, "We look before and after, and pine for what is not." We are like the people arriving at the Grand Canyon on a tour bus, so busy chatting with each other about the places they have been to and the places they are heading for next, as to be completely oblivious to the landmark before them.

Some people are so driven by time that they cannot relax and enjoy themselves. You have seen them casting anxious glances, at concert hall, theater, movie, gymnasium, or nightclub, at their watches. They do so two or three times an hour—during the intermission, during the performance, during the applause; they exhibit openly their inability to let their hair down, to forget their past commitments and future needs, to enjoy the present and to let "now" take them out of time altogether. The wristwatch is the shackle of an invisible chain that binds them in slavery to the great devouring god Time, and their glances at it are so many obeisances to an icon.

Many people spend their lives looking forward. "When I'm nine years old, I'll be allowed to do the wild things that my brother is allowed to do, like stay up as late as eight o'clock, cross the street by myself, open the refrigerator." Then you look forward to being in that awesome place called elementary school and, when that pleasure fades, in high school. Then to being in college, away from home and parents and from restrictions on your personal life. Next you look forward to graduate or professional school or to being financially independent. Then to establishing yourself in a job or practice, to marrying and starting families.

Then the same cycle starts on behalf of your children. As a new parent, you eagerly await the days when the kid will be out of the diaper and crying period. Then you anticipate the end of the dependency period; it seems the child is always running in front of cars or falling down the stairs. Next you look forward to the years when you can talk to your offspring adult to adult and not have to get on his or her immature level and play games.

You are oblivious all the while that looking at your children only in terms of obnoxious periods to get through is a fallacy. As a proverb has it, "Small kids, small problems; big kids, big problems." When this member of the next generation reaches maturity and the time for those dreamed-of adult-to-adult talks, he or she has become rebellious and alienated. Crossing the generation gap, your child has practically walked out of his or her parents' lives; and there is nothing left you except wonderment about what happened to all the other years. *Why did you wish them away and on behalf of what things that never materialized? And what happened to your whole life of wishing things away on behalf*

*of some exciting prospect in the future? You never enjoyed each
stage of parenthood.*

Great expectations

No matter how well you may be doing in your vocational life, you are not satisfied either. You have hopes and
expectations. You never rest on your laurels. In one sense,
that is very good. Such dissatisfaction keeps you striving,
brings you new worlds to conquer, and accounts for many
of mankind's finest achievements. In another sense, it is
bad, because it means that you never enjoy the present,
never fully enjoy what you have achieved with so large an
investment of aspiration, money, time, and struggle.

Many people live, like Charles Dickens's immortal Mr.
Micawber, always waiting for something to turn up. Some
day, possibly tomorrow, their ship will come in. Their winning lottery ticket will solve their problems; not just financial problems but *all* problems, for money from a distance
seems like a good solvent.

Some have so refined the art of great expectations
that the high point of their lives every day is what is called
in the army, "mail call." Until the mail carrier arrives, the
day is full of promise, whether or not the sun shines. Anything can happen and most likely will, and of course it is
bound to be good. When only bills and those inevitable so-
licitations arrive, the rest of the day is shot. Just another
bunch of boring routines and a lot of disagreeable work to
get through. But at least there is tomorrow's mail call to
look forward to, and by evening hope swells again.

Do you recognize yourself in this description? If you do,
you have an ailment: Futuritis. Always living for the days
to come and being out of touch with the present. You are

like the old Brooklyn Dodger fan who perennially said, "Wait till next year."

Look at the recent bicentennial celebration—how long the preparations took and how the talk about it and the excitement grew. It was years in the making, occupying the lives of numerous officials. How quickly it passed, especially that climactic July 4. How soon forgotten, the mementos gathering dust. This is typical of so much in individual as well as communal life.

Being frozen into the past

PASTITIS

Futuritis is a disease that afflicts young people and remains with most modern people to the end of their days. Its sister disease is Pastitis. Many stories have been written about people like Dickens's Miss Havisham. Stood up on her wedding day, she spent the rest of her life in her wedding dress, living in the room where the ceremony was to have taken place, with everything set up as it had been for that day, including the wedding cake, and with the clock stopped at the moment when she was jilted. This extreme case etches brilliantly a common enough mentality—being frozen into the past, having eyes directed backwards.

Just as Futuritis is strongest in the early years, so Pastitis is strongest in the later stages of life. Yet it begins early enough. According to some psychologists, you grow up with a nostalgia for the warmth and simplicity of the womb or for the first days of infancy when the whole universe was an extension of yourself or consisted mainly of your mother's breast.

Then, despite the friskiness and relative freedom of being with one's friends, you think back, when beset by members of your rat pack or by demanding teachers, to the days of early childhood, the days you were—or so it seems now—free as the wind, did as you pleased, and lived in the security of the family nest. With each step forward into maturity, responsibility, and complexity, there seems to be a concomitant loss of innocence, simplicity, harmony. Mature people accept those losses. Many people are not mature, and in them the result is nostalgia, regret, or fixation on the past.

The older you become, the more your climaxes accumulate behind rather than in front of you and the more you may look back nostalgically to the good old days that were. You contemplate the successes you had, or you impute success to events that were in fact indifferent in quality. You regret the defeats, mistakes, and missed opportunities. Everyone is in some way arrested, like Miss Havisham, in some stage of psychological development. Someone once said that many people die at twenty-five and are buried forty years later. No longer aware of current events, they see themselves through the haze of the past. The college student still talks about her achievements in high school, and the old sports fan thinks that baseball reached a climax with the World Series of 1940 or 1950—when he was young and at the climax of *his* life— and has been going downhill ever since.

In fact, the everyday talk about how terrible everything has become is rooted in Pastitis. Generals, it has often been remarked, prepare for the last war; and one of the reasons that the world is in such a mess may be that it changes rapidly, but the politicians and the electorate who put them into power are unable to keep up with the changes; they bring tired old solutions to unprecedented situations.

Only the present

WHAT CAN BE DONE?

So it is that you are likely to be dreaming of that home run you hit with bases loaded at age eight and never duplicated or to be still kicking yourself for not having gone to a different college when you were seventeen. At the same time, your emotions are heavily invested also in the future, in the form of hopes and ambitions. Being like the Roman god Janus, with one face in either direction, leaves little energy and attention for the present. No wonder it gets such short shrift. That is the problem.

No easy solution exists, but at least knowing the nature of the problem helps. Getting yourself to live in the present is probably impossible in pure form. One should become at least a little less past and future oriented and thereby, if only by default, leave more room for the present.

What, then, can you do positively? Consider it minutely. Are you living for sex, or winning the lottery, or going to London as the supreme value? Orgasms last briefly, and a person who lives mainly for sex therefore confronts the problem of having much time to kill between bouts of lovemaking. He or she looks back to the last great orgasm and eagerly awaits the next one.

You may choose to live for sex and put up with the interludes as necessary gaps of time to be gotten through as painlessly as possible. You may also, and perhaps more

wisely, see the glass as half full rather than half empty—
and live for other things than sex. These other things will
occupy your time, and you can let sex be the grace note of
life, the added touch. *Getting to London may be as much fun as
being in London.* Hence you can concentrate on something
like a career or school, on meaningful work, long-range
plans. Sex is not crowded out; it is supplemented.

For another thing, stop using history and politics as a
cop-out, a gripe, an escape. There are no "good old days";
and if you stop playing the "grass is greener" game, you
can simplify the unsettled conditions of your epoch by
simply changing the way you see things, by discarding cli-
chés and starting to think. If the present will in turn be regarded by future generations as the "good old days," what
a shame that you cannot enjoy it instead of looking to the
"good old days" in the past and to the Utopia that progress
will bring in the future. *Stop contrasting a half-understood
present with a fabulous past and a nebulous future.* Stop worrying
in vain, and start enjoying the "good old days" now while
you have them, that is, while you are alive. *Whatever period
your body finds itself in is the "good old days," and you had better
bring your mind along.* Remember that, in one sense, as far
as your body is concerned, there is no past or future, only
the present. Make your mind come along with that reality
at least a little bit. End the schism between a solidly rooted
body, which has a wisdom of its own on this matter, and an
erratic, roving, dissatisfied, confused mind—ever-com-
paring, calculating (that is, miscalculating) and complaining. *Give your body a chance by giving your mind a rest.*

19

Living in the Present

Create your experiences

A religious man once said that it is a good deed to go to the zoo every six months. Though his remark had a religious thrust, it remains relevant to nonreligious people. You should go to the zoo, because it is one of the things in our everyday world that can forcefully jolt you out of the tracks of the commonplace, pedestrian, habitual. Most people go there as children, as parents (when they take their own children), and again as grandparents. A quarter century between visits is a shame.

You probably wonder how doing a "childish" thing like going to a zoo can alter your life. But it is not childish at all. It is one accessible gateway to delight. Not having recently visited it, you have long forgotten how special an experience it is to see the sheer awesomeness and diversity of creation; the infinite combinations of faces, colors, lines,

222

and life traits in creatures that fly, run, or crawl. When you become too overwhelmed by habit, too beaten down by grief, too wrapped up in your personal concerns, discover at zoo or aquarium the marvel of the world around you.

You pass through the gates and suddenly find yourself in Africa and Asia, in wilderness and jungle and tropical river. You are in a world without cities, football teams, beer ads, gas stations, buildings, or land cultivation, a world prehistoric and prehuman. To the religious man, the zoo was the book of God's works, a manifestation of God's resourcefulness, love of beauty, and generosity in creating everything imaginable and giving humanity a vivid domicile. The majesty of eagle, lion, and tiger ("Tiger, tiger, burning bright"); the menacing stare of the serpent; the gracefulness of gazelle; the exotic ugliness of rhinoceros or hippopotamus; the touching vulnerability of lamb and small birds; the lumbering dignity of elephant or bear; the peculiar charms of giraffe, monkey, ostrich—it is all a gallery that outdoes the dreams of the greatest writers, painters, or symphonists.

The nonreligious visitor need not refer anything to God; for, no matter what your theory of creation, you are struck by the beauty of the given world. The excursion is into magic, *the magic of reality. Except for some stray association with childhood experiences in the zoo, you think little about past or future, career or personal life.* You are awestruck, reverent, transported. And *that* is living in the present.

You have been taken out of yourself. Or, it should more fairly be said that you have been taken *into* yourself. That deepest and best self has confronted the world around you, whereas in your everyday life it is imprisoned in a little corner of the world, in a cell created by the tribalisms you cling to, the masks you put on, and the friends and habits you limit yourself to. You have now been dazzled out of "thought" and into thought—out of conventional, habitual, practical thought and into philosophical, lyrical, imaginative, creative thought. You seem to have traveled to another world when all you have done is entered your own world, so badly cut off from it have you been in your everyday life. And by realizing that the world does not rotate around you, the herd you run with, or the tribe you belong to, and that time is not governed by the calendar, the clock, or the cities and institutions of man, you are in the present. You are, in your humble way, like the greatest explorer, adventurer, hunter.

In the following pages we present a series of experiences that are available to all of us, if we only open ourselves to them.

Twinkle, twinkle, little star

Another profound experience, that of the no less incredible marvels of the cosmos, is available as near as your planetarium—or your backyard. For you need not go anywhere. Just step outside your home on a clear night and gaze at the sky. Clusters of stars are so thick that they seem to be clouds. All that the naked eye can see is but a small portion of the *known* part of the universe. It consists of billions of galaxies, each of which contains billions of stars like our sun, around many of which revolve numerous planets like the earth. Out there are such large numbers, such infinite time, such vast areas of the profoundest darkness and cold as well as the most unimaginable brilliance of light and heat.

Just look at those stars for a minute or two. Ignore all

practical considerations that some bring to them—hikers and sea voyagers worrying over their own location, astronomers worrying over constellations and stellar theories. Forget tomorrow's work or last week's fiasco. Give yourself to the sheer experience. Put yourself outside time, outside yourself. Lost in the infinity and eternity of the universe that those stars embody, let your awe and sense of mystery overwhelm you. The experience is as good as any "high" from alcohol or drugs.

Look at an individual star shimmering. It is far, far away. Through how many billions of miles and millions of years; through what dark spaces—silent, without motion—those rays traveled from what vast star many times the size of the sun before finally registering on those small orbs called your eyes? How strange it all is. *How insignificant suddenly seem the worries you have about next week or the last one.* What a mystery the universe is, with its explosive quality; its myriad of concurrent motions at unbelievable speeds; its unthinkable extent of darkness, silence. Now there is food for thought! But how many adults—is it even one in a thousand or ten thousand?—think those thoughts—of surprise, delight, awe—once in a lifetime? And yet there is the catalyst right beside you, outside your very door or window, requiring no money or mobility. Such is the blinding tyranny of habit that, for most people, that catalyst might as well be thousands of miles away.

"Where do I fit into all this? What does it all mean? Where are we all going?" These are unanswerable questions generated by such sky-staring. Are they disturbing because unanswerable? In a way, but in a good way. They excite us with a sense of wonder. And of wisdom: Why hassle yourself and others? Why not just relax and take it all in, absorb the universe in your consciousness? There is no outside; everywhere is one gigantic room. You are at home anywhere.

For a brief while, you have been taken outside yourself. You have undergone a supernatural feeling in being able to encounter the universe visually and mentally. You have had the mystic experience known to religious persons or hippies. Instead of going through arduous religious discipline, prayer, contemplation, and fasting, or going to legally and medically dubious devices like drugs, you had the experience by a simple visit to the planetarium or your backyard.

Most people all the time and some people most of the time go through life marooned in the daily trivia and the immediate environment. Theirs is a world exclusively of dirty streets, run-down buildings, noisy subways, traffic-jammed streets, and the pressured, dull job. *It is as if someone visiting the Metropolitan Opera, the Metropolitan Museum of Art, the National Gallery, or the Louvre were to spend all the time there studying the fine print on the entrance ticket.*

LANDSCAPING

Or try looking at a sunset or, an even rarer experience, a sunrise. When was the last time you did so? For most people, many years ago. Here is an experience that takes place almost every day and, like the other experiences we talked about, is free. The color of the clouds, the movement of the sun, the changes it causes in the human bustle—all that can be appreciated anywhere. Soak in the beauty of the experience, whether in conjunction with the calm of a city dawn or with the tumult of people rushing home. Then go for a change to mountaintop or lakeside, and see the spectacle there.

What of the seasonal colors? When was the last time you went out of your way to look at the flowers and blossoms in the spring, the many-colored leaves in the fall, the white carpeting in the dead of winter? Try it. On your train ride in to work every day, you possibly bury your head in the morning newspaper and tell yourself that next fall, when you are less busy, you will look out the window, instead, or make a photography excursion. But you have been telling yourself that for years; it's *always* next year. Stop it. Make *this* the year, the month, the day. Get up and take a ride, a hike, a tour. It costs very little, and you may find that there is a lot more to it than you ever suspected.

Travel

Travel is another great wrencher of habit and therefore recharger of batteries. You need not travel abroad; this is a huge country, and there are places you have not been to. Not the packaged travel with tour, guides, itineraries mapped out months earlier, and insulated buses filled with fellow travelers going to famous sites observed for fifteen minutes; not these, but travel on your own, with few bookings, itineraries, tours guides. If "adventure" is defined as a journey with no clear destination, travel can be adventure. At the least, it is an escape from the deadening habits and routines of every workday and every week.

You wake up in a strange city or country, hearing novel sounds. A whole city is to be explored, savored, seen from every angle. The day is not mapped out in any way—no schedule, appointment, destination. You feel free as a lark. You can go any way you choose at the moment of going, do anything you think of on the spot.

An ancient sage said that no matter what land you

come to, you are always under the same sky. His point was
that you cannot run away from your problems. True
enough, and nicely put, too. Yet his remark must not be
taken too literally. Travel, to be sure, is not the panacea. It
is not—any more than are drugs, religious conversion, or
money—a permanent escape. On the other hand, it gives
you a refreshing interlude of freedom from the prison of
routine. And it can bring you back to school, job, and
habits with a new vigor, a higher degree of tolerance, a
greater perceptivity and appreciation of things as they are
and as they perhaps must remain.

A NEW SET OF EYES

How about taking up painting or photography? You
need not be a master. Just do it to enjoy yourself, not to
impress anyone. You will not only have a good time, but
you will discover that the process educates your eye. You
become much more sensitive to the sheer appearance of
things. You notice the texture of materials and objects all
about you; you notice the play of light, the infinite gradations of colors, the shapes and outlines of objects, the
changes of perspective, the relativity of size, the way in
which things interact with each other. As everything becomes, through habit, domesticated, flattened out,
simplified—nothing less than the freshness and openness
of the painter's eye can take apart the universe around you
and recompose it as if from scratch.

This new mode of seeing also opens you to the world
of art, to an appreciation of what other artists were and are
trying to do. Painting may lead you to museum visits, or
sometimes museum visits may lead you to painting; or the
two go on concurrently. A fine arts museum is to many

people as dreary as a mausoleum. As long as they continue their normal way of life, it will remain so. But if perusal of this book leads you to a reexamination of premises, an alteration of life-style, a disruption of habits, experiments in new values—the idea of such a visit may no longer be so repellent. Take a second look at a museum. You may still hate it. That is all right; at least you made sure. Then again, there is just a chance that you may see it with different eyes.

If you do, you have no idea how many new doorways and adventures it may open for you. Give it a try; all that it can cost you is one afternoon and a couple of dollars. You have surely spent more, much more, than that on futile attempts to jazz up your life. At the worst, consider this as one more—and a simple, inexpensive—attempt to do so.

THE SOUND OF MUSIC AND OF WORDS

While you are giving museums another chance, why not the same with concert halls? Many people have unhappy recollections of being forced by a well-meaning teacher or relative to attend a concert. Again think of the changes you may have undergone in other areas of life without having checked whether such changes apply as well to aural experience. Is it not possible that you might find, if you only gave yourself the opportunity, that you enjoy different music now than you did when you were younger?

Go where your taste takes you. Don't worry about who's great and who isn't. Such things take care of themselves. You might want to precede, supplement, or follow your concert going by listening to classical music stations and records. Write down the names of pieces of music that you like. Go out of your way to hear those pieces again and again. Then move on to related pieces. If there is any kind of movement, you will be delighted at how quickly so vast a world of pleasure, hitherto completely untapped, has suddenly opened to you. Sounds themselves will become a source of wonderment, just as sights are to the artist's eyes.

Besides looking at new things or looking at old things newly, you can *think* in fresh ways, meaning *reading* in fresh ways. Visit libraries—those museums of words, concert halls of ideas—scattered all over the city and in each town. Schooling has for many people just about destroyed the experience of reading a serious book. The assignments were forced on you; you had to go at the pace the teacher wanted; you had to write dreary reports on them; you were tested on them; the subject may not have interested you; the style seemed stiff and formal; the reading had to compete with movies, TV, basketball, and social clubs. You could hardly imagine a more obnoxious way of being introduced to anything. You probably swore on graduating that you would never again open a book, and most people make that one of the few vows they keep.

Take another look at the situation. Give yourself another chance. Try now any book that might interest you. It may lead to others, and the process of going from one book to another may lead you out of the field of interest you began with. A book on astronomy or zoology can bring you to theology or philosophy. Or use current events as a starting point. Is the Middle East or South Africa on the verge of war, and do you have a moderate interest in what is going on there? Try a history of the place. Did the president in his last speech or news conference quote Abe Lincoln? How much do you know about that remarkable —and by no means saintly—man, who is for many non-

Americans the quintessential American? Why not try a biography of him? Or, if you like war movies, a biography of Patton, of Napoleon or Hitler, of Lee or Grant?

If you saw a movie version recently of a well-known classic like *The Great Gatsby* or *Great Expectations*, try reading it. Are you upset by the tendency of churches to appoint women as ministers? Read up a little on early Christianity; you might find it to be a fascinating subject. Or try some anthropology on the place of women in various societies. Do you marvel at the breakthroughs in the sciences—the DNA theory in biology, the theory of relativity in physics, the black holes in astronomy, the Oedipus complex in psychology? Take a look at a history of the discipline or at a popularizing explanation.

Reading will also have a decided effect on one of your key habits—your assumptions about many things. Most people secure their supposed hold on the truth by reading only those things that reinforce their values. This parochialism and cave dwelling is common even among advanced and enlightened persons. Think of those who gave themselves so readily to the enthusiasms of World War I, or of Hitler's expeditions, of the Vietnam adventure, and who lived to regret having participated in delusion, deception, and injustice. That should make you think twice about your own commitments and enthusiasms, your own unexamined assumptions.

Thinking about things like that may also introduce you to, or should go hand in hand with, thinking about many other things. One poet spoke of seeing "a world in a grain of sand, an eternity in an hour." What he meant was that to any probing mind, even the most minute, humble, or ugly object can become the heart of the universe. If you but think through every aspect, you will find that everything ties in with everything else; any object has a common denominator with any other. Insofar as you master the universals of human behavior, you can be said to have tamed eternity, put it under the microscope, reduced it to proportion. Any hour of life then becomes the microcosm of all other hours, any act or object becomes a complex interconnection of everything, and eternity becomes merely an infinitely repeated sine curve of basic events and attitudes. You never cease to marvel at the fascinating things of this world, the infinitely variable and colorful entities, the interplay of similarity and difference, of predictable and unpredictable, of unique and universal, even in the same individual, object, or event. This is no momentary discovery but a vision that grows on you during a lifetime and that requires constant reapplication and development, confirmation and modification. Enough is there to keep you occupied and delighted all day long and all life long.

EAT, JOG, AND BE MERRY

When was the last time you enjoyed your food or were even conscious of it? "Oh, it's good," you say to the cook and resume conversation, oblivious to what you have consumed. Do spend less time talking so much, and let each of your experiences sink in. That food will taste much better once you make it a part of your consciousness as well as of your mouth.

What about that body of yours, of which the food will become a part? Do you wear it proudly or like an old rag? Do you slouch or walk tall? Do you let yourself turn fat, clumsy, and unattractive? Do you care what you put into it, or use it as a garbage can? Why not start caring?

What about exercising as a way of helping you keep in

shape? (Get a checkup and the OK from your doctor first, of course.) It is a good way of improving muscle tone, physique, blood pressure, pride. Do all the "ups"—push-ups, sit-ups, jump-ups, pull-ups—slowly at first, then every day. Five or ten minutes of it. Increase and improve every day. Start jogging. Not hard running, just jogging or even fast walking. Not to the point of losing your breath, just to the point of increasing your breath and heartbeat.

You don't have to do the marathon's twenty-six miles at four minutes per. Not at the start, anyway. Just begin by doing a ten or fifteen-minute mile, or even half mile. Do that daily for weeks. Move up only slowly. There is no rush. It took you years to run your body down; it will take months to turn that around. You might, after a year or so, find yourself doing three miles in twenty minutes and, after another year, five miles in a half hour. That's damn good, but you don't have to do that at all. You can keep on doing a mile in ten minutes. Just do it every day or, by way of compromise, every nonrainy day when the temperature is anywhere between twenty and eighty-five degrees.

At first it will hurt and annoy, and you will wish for it to be over. Soon enough, you will get used to it. You will experience getting your second wind. You will encounter the sheer pleasure of moving smoothly, confidently. You will enjoy the vistas, especially if you can do it in a nearby park, of the trees in each season. You will find yourself solving problems and thinking original thoughts. You will relish for a change inhaling deep draughts of oxygen instead of carbon mon- or dioxide. You will possess a body loose and free. You will enjoy having the body respond to your will, having it precede your thoughts rather than trudge wearily behind. You will enjoy slimming it down and using it as a delicate instrument, instead of having it be a clog. You will enjoy the agility, the rhythmic activity. You will enjoy breathing deep and being alive. You will enjoy the present.

That jogging initially is hard work should be no deterrent. After all, life is filled with readily available, simple pleasures lurking behind discomfort. Think of the delight you feel when you are thirsty and get your mouth to a drink—any sort of drink, including so humble a thing as a glass of water. For a minute you are all throat, no mind, no consciousness.

Too many of us feel that we are such fragile souls that we cannot tolerate any sort of adversity. We put water coolers and stores dispensing drinks everywhere to make sure that no one ever gets thirsty. By avoiding an uncomfortable experience, however, we miss out on a rich experience. Sometimes it makes sense to go a little thirsty or hungry ("appetite," it is then called) for the pleasure of stopping. You don't know how good it is until you miss it. So too the pleasure of jogging and, above all, of having jogged easily redeem the pain and inconvenience of starting to jog.

TALK IS CHEAP, TOO CHEAP

How are you relating to people these days? It has been suggested that the average married couple speak to each other an average of twenty-seven minutes a week. Clearly, the nature of your relationships to your friends or spouse has changed drastically and imperceptibly over the years. One way of reviving your life would be to become aware of that alteration and to try to reverse it.

How is your talking in general these days? Maybe you should, if you are not the shy type, shut up for a change.

Have you ever noticed how most conversation consists of monologues by the participants, who do not listen to each other? As a matter of fact, here is a nice bit of consciousness raising or game playing that you might try: Next time you are in a conversation with a group of people, detach yourself mentally from it, and listen carefully even as you continue your own reduced contribution to the talk. Notice how little people listen to each other, how each one is continuing on his or her own little tangent, regardless of whether anyone else responds or cares. Notice how when Jones says of Smith that he is a great conversationalist, what he really means is not that Smith has any profound things to say but that Smith listens to what Jones says.

For better relating, then, try to put a little less of your griping into your conversation. Listen more, and respond to what the other people say. It may not interest you, but surely some aspect of it may relate to your interests; with that common denominator, that bridge, real dialogue can begin.

Your friend, for instance, is trying to get into graduate school; she talks about the competition and the forms she has to fill out for admission. You never went beyond high school and have no interest in admission committees, nor do you care about the agonies of applying to schools. Yet surely some interest must be held in common—say, the problems faced in undertaking new things. That is something that your friend is finding out about and that you experienced when you got your first job. Start talking about that as soon as you tactfully can.

Or take your friend, the home owner; he rambles on about all the headaches and conveniences of home owning. You are a confirmed apartment dweller and could not care less about the agonies and ecstasies of owning your own home. Yet, you have a common interest, the problem of the maximum use of space. That is something that both the home owner and the apartment dweller are faced with. Your home owner friend will be glad to give you the benefits of his numerous experiences, and you will have found a subtopic dear to you. Any two subjects under the sun, and therefore any two conversationalists, can be tied together provided that the common denominator is found and injected into the talk.

Consider also doing nothing at all for a change. When was the last time you did that? If you are to master yourself by becoming more active and vigorous, such periods of doing should be balanced by periods of passivity and relaxation, of letting reality soak into your consciousness. Be concurrently more active and leisurely.

What have you learned?

The contact with eternity made possible by zoo, planetarium, and travel, no less than the delights of museum, book, gourmet dining, jogging, and conversing, will be an end in itself. It is not going to solve any of your problems. It will do something more important. It will transcend them, give you a perspective on them, let you see them perhaps as basically not problems at all. It will add a new dimension to your life. This vacation from everyday reality, from the movielike illusions of everyday life on earth, is really a trip to the ultimate reality.

Looking at everything from up close, acting as if everything involves the decline and fall of the universe, is a big part of many people's problems. Keep things in perspective. Remember that this too—all of it—shall pass.

Sure, the things matter while you are in the here and now, but you live not only in the here and now. We are amphibians of a sort—partly in one medium, partly in the other. To not care about joys and sorrows, victories and defeats, is to be too much in eternity; to get too carried away by them is to be too much in time. You have to perform a great balancing act.

LIVING EACH DAY FOR ITS OWN SAKE

Doing things with a heightened consciousness of the larger universe around you enhances your appreciation of everything and every moment. "Thank God for my ailments," a sage has exclaimed, and it is true that when you begin to take the pleasures of everyday life too much for granted and spend too much time griping over trivia, it takes only a flu—which flattens you for a few days and enervates you for a week or two—to make you appreciate the sheer joy of merely rising in the morning, walking down the street hale and hearty, savoring even a homely meal. There is nothing like being deprived of something to make you feel how much you love and need it.

A wise individual will treasure defeats and sufferings for what they make him or her appreciate the more; he or she will chalk many things up to experience. A wiser person, with active mind, will come to that understanding without having to undergo loss and deprivation and before it is too late to profit from the lesson.

Once venturing upon an intellectual encounter with the universe, do you not then become fully conscious of being alive, of the joy of living? Merely to live is the greatest triumph, and every part of life becomes enveloped by a shimmering halo. The preciousness that life then takes on makes you newly aware of its transience, even as awareness of its transience makes you aware of its preciousness.

Medieval holy men and thinkers used to keep skulls on their desks as a reminder that death always lurked around the corner. "What if this were the world's last night?" asked a poet; and in the nuclear age, his question has renewed potency and relevance. The purpose of such reminders in the old days was to make the Christian soul prepared to meet its Maker. Knowing that at any moment you could die and be judged for eternity was a spur to your living a good life and avoiding the perils of damnation.

For nonreligious people, such a prospect is not credible. Death is still with us, nevertheless, and extinction is no less a stimulant for present intense living than is the fear of judgment. One way of improving the quality of your life, therefore, is to live as if you were under sentence of death. And so, indeed we all are, but we have received postponements of execution of varying lengths. Some of us will make the exit tomorrow, others fifty years from now. The reminder of the common doom is bracing. It should suffice to have you make every hour count.

A checklist

One way of making it count is to periodically consult a checklist of basics: Are you in good health? Do you have people you love and who, with all your faults and despite various moods, still love you? Are you doing what you like? Are you planning for your future by preparing yourself in school? Do you have brothers, sisters, cousins, parents, and friends who—when all headaches are taken account of—are a plus in your life? Do your car and appliances more or less function properly?

If the answer to most or all of these questions is "yes," and yet you gripe, you are a Conniptor. Do not engage in self-pity and self-indulgence, for as most people in this world go, you are a highly fortunate person. Anything you complain about is superficial. *Where is your sense of perspective? Your glass is not half empty—it is nine-tenths full!*

20

Conclusion

Looking at where we have been

Let us look back now to see how far we have come. We have offered a sketch of the universal human difficulties, the varying admixtures of which go to form each person's peculiar problem. In the most general terms, that means that you may have difficulty coping because you do not know yourself (Part One) and because you neither possess nor desire the truth about anything (Part Two). These two basic handicaps create equally serious subsidiary problems in the way you think (Part Three). Making your way back to effectiveness and clarity requires various changes in mental and physical habits (Part Four).

Though for the purposes of analysis, we took them up in a logical sequence, these problems often combine and recombine in the complex network of people and things that is reality. You face, in essence, only one or a few problems seen from different angles. Thus consciousness of mixed motives and feelings of inferiority are in a chicken-and-egg relationship. Feelings of aloneness, like those of inferiority, beget feelings of superiority, the compulsion to join organizations, and fanaticism about one's beliefs. They result also in contempt for those who would hold up the mirror to your face, envy of those who seem to be doing better than you, and griping about everybody and everything. You wait for lightning to strike while you spend your money and time accumulating unnecessary possessions, adding responsibilities, and wallowing in trivia rather than confronting yourself or the magic world around you. You let childish traits and vested interests, words and unacknowledged feelings—especially wishes and fears—shape your habits and assumptions, which in turn blind you to the possibility of alternate life-styles. You live in the past or the future—anywhere but in the present. You thereby reduce the present to being a fleeting, joyless instant, and you rush through life a prisoner of habit, of many bad habits.

Finding time, purging your misunderstandings, and undertaking any of the suggested changes requires a single, albeit at first wrenching, change. It is, in a sense, the only change you will have to make, because it will break open a dam—and then get out of the way! That change is, *break the habits. Break the habit of habits.* That done, all other changes will easily follow. To that end, *any* change is good, regardless of what is being changed or how. Change for change's sake can work miracles. Then you will find yourself ready to live in the present, which means ready to live.

How do you break habits? You hardly need to be told to eat, drink, and be merry. But some need advice on how to make those actions as fresh as if they were created anew today. Such refinements can make the simple acts truly and recurringly satisfying and relatively lasting. But first you must locate yourself in time.

Learn to discard a lot of the unnecessary baggage that you travel with through life. Discard the baggage of the past—the fact that others made and shaped you. Discard the baggage of the present—the attempt to live by and for the dreamworld of advertisements; to pursue the goals and life-styles of others; to reflect yourself in the approval of others; to impress others. Discard the baggage of the future—the demand that you selflessly sacrifice yourself for an elusive future.

When it comes to other people, with their attitudes, demands, fashions, and expectations, only one slogan is relevant: Don't give a damn. *Don't give a damn what others will say or think*—once you have made sure that they are wrong.

Another point that bears repetition is that anxiety is perfectly normal. What can, however, be done is to reduce an inordinate amount of anxiety to a healthy norm, and that is what the suggestions in this book are about.

The reduction of anxiety is possible through a fundamental realization, which is that *you are not alone*. If you feel terribly inferior and inadequate, terribly alone, terribly guilty over petty, vindictive, lustful, sadistic, or selfish thoughts, that is because you believe that you alone harbor such horrors, while the rest of mankind thinks only the thoughts that they express, only the good clean official rhetoric with which we belabor each other in conversation and speeches.

But if there is anything this book has to teach you, it is that *everyone*—saint, hero, or sinner—thinks these dishonorable-seeming thoughts. Relax, therefore. You are—like everyone else—normal, healthy, and average, not at all an eccentric. Go on from where you are, and do what you want, become what you can, and don't look back at your thoughts. Live with them. They will take care of themselves. They will never go away, no matter what you do. Just leave them to themselves, and turn yourself to what you can become. *Stop agonizing over* THOUGHTS, *and start doing* THINGS.

Is that what it's all about?

You may say that some of our little self-improvement projects are trivial and cover only a small area of everyday life. True, *but put them all together and see what you have!* Your whole day is covered. The way you eat your meal, the way you read your newspaper, the way you talk to people at home, at work, on the phone; the way you spend your spare time, what you do with yourself—virtually everything will have been affected. Each item is only one brick, yet even the biggest brick buildings can be erected only one brick at a time. As you begin with each activity, it may seem small in itself; but before you know it, the amalgamation of them has altered your way of life; and you may have become a different, happier person.

All these things are simple and within your reach; most are inexpensive. Not to at least sample them is worse than a blunder and almost a crime. The poet Robert Frost once wrote a poem about a farmer who lived near a mysterious magical spring atop a mountain but never bothered to visit it. So do many of us live next to great places and experiences and never even know them or take advantage of them.

If you act, question, experiment, no longer will your life seem to drift, without destination or compass, without hope or aspiration or expectation. You will know the joy of shaping your life, instead of having it shaped for you by others and by circumstances. Instead of feeling helpless and Jell-O-like; shaking with every tremor in the environment; being shapeless, transparent, bland; you will be a person with your own tastes and with an individuality, an identity carved out of the bedrock of life experience, out of the wrenching of old and commonplace habits. *You have entered upon a new life.*

Just remember that when you have mastered the joy of sex, the joy of cooking, the joy of conversation, the joy of history, the joy of hobbies, the joy of travel, the joy of thinking, the joy of running, the joy of laughter, you will have raised your consciousness—not just in any one field, but in every way. You will have learned the joy of joy. The joy of life.

The key to your predicament, it bears repeating, is that most of your difficulties have to do not with the way *things are externally* but with the way *you feel internally*, not with your environment and circumstances but with your assumptions and misconceptions, *not with the state of things but with the direction of your thoughts about them.*

That is a quandary, moreover, in which *you are not alone, special, different.* Nor will you feel that a way out is possible as long as you remain a prisoner of your mental habits—that is, your assumptions. Once you break the habits of everyday life and, more important, start questioning your unexamined assumptions, you will, like a climber reaching a mountaintop, see all sorts of new vistas.

The central theme of this book and the single most important thing you can do is to break your habits, both physical and mental. Your change of assumptions will not affect the physical world around you—at first. But just wait. From some small habit broken because of a raised question and an examined assumption, has come the transformation of the world—by men like Abraham, Moses, Buddha, Socrates, Jesus, Mohammed, Marx, Lincoln, Mao. So begin to question.

The vast majority of people can change. They have only one or two serious deficiencies. But they have to face their predicament squarely: Either remedy their deficiency, or, writing it off as a loss, turn instead to concentrating on their strengths. The choice is yours—would you rather improve what is weak or focus on what is strong? We would not venture to tell you which course to take. What we do advise most strongly is that everyone face this fork in the road of life; the sooner they face it and act on it, the better off they will be.

Don't look back, as the old ball player–sage said. Don't worry about the years you may have misspent. Once you have broken through to a new outlook, the temptation will be strong to say to yourself, "Oh, my God, why didn't I do that years ago!" Then you will be right back where you were, living in the past, wallowing in regret, envy, nostalgia, self-dissatisfaction; taking refuge in emotional baths rather than action. No, far better *to rejoice that the change came at all and that it came now rather than years from now!*

You must see that this is, as the saying popular a decade ago had it, *the first day of the rest of your life*. Living as if you were to die tomorrow, as if this were the last day of your life, transforms this day, miraculously, into the first day of the rest of your life. And should that life be fated to be long, it may now also turn out to be rich.

You say that many of these changes, insofar as they

involve breaking lifelong assumptions and habits, are hard? What of that? Do you recall how hard learning to drive a car, or even learning the alphabet, once seemed? There were moments when you despaired of success; yet look at you now. *Everything in life seems hard, at first. And nothing really is, at last.*

Your new approach to life is a world newly discovered, a regeneration, a conversion, a second birth, another chance, a dawn, an awakening.

Good Morning!

Index